first time
QUILTING

Creative Publishing international

First published in the United States of America by
Creative Publishing international, a member of
Quarto Publishing Group USA Inc.
400 First Avenue North
Suite 400
Minneapolis, MN 55401
1-800-328-3895
www.creativepub.com
Visit www.Craftside.Typepad.com for a behind-the-scenes peek at our crafty world!

ISBN: 978-1-58923-824-4

Digital edition published in 2014
eISBN: 978-1-62788-224-8

10 9 8 7 6 5 4 3 2 1

Library of Congress Cataloging-in-Publication Data available

Cover Design, Book Design, and Page Layout: Megan Jones Design
Illustrations: Heather Lambert
Photographs: CPi and Rau + Barber
Cover Photography: Shutterstock.com
Printed in China

first time

QUILTING

THE ABSOLUTE BEGINNER'S GUIDE

by the editors of Creative Publishing international

Creative Publishing
international

contents

introduction

WELCOME TO THE FUN AND REWARDING WORLD OF QUILTING. *FIRST TIME QUILTING* IS DESIGNED TO ENCOURAGE CREATIVITY AND INSTILL CONFIDENCE AS YOU LEARN TO SEW AND QUILT. EASY-TO-FOLLOW INSTRUCTIONS WITH COLORFUL PHOTOGRAPHS AND ILLUSTRATIONS HELP YOU BUILD YOUR SEWING SKILLS WHILE MAKING USEFUL AND APPEALING QUILTED HOME DECORATING ITEMS AND ACCESSORIES.

Quilting, once a necessary household activity, is now considered an art form. The color combinations and patterns are limited only by your imagination. Many quilters prefer traditional block patterns, but quilts also can be designed in modern, bold, or whimsical styles to complement any décor. If you're learning to sew, quilting is a great way to hone your skills of cutting, piecing, pressing, and stitching with accuracy. And there's no need to purchase expensive fabrics; you may find a purpose for even the smallest pieces of leftover material.

This book will teach you, step-by-step, how to make great-looking quilted items while you're learning the fundamentals of sewing. The eleven quilting projects provide a sampling of quilt block patterns, techniques, and styles. With each project you'll learn new skills. You will also find tips and explanations throughout the book to help you understand the reason behind the instructions. And while the projects suggest size and color combinations, the possibilities are endless. Experiment with your own designs and fabric choices.

Use the first section of the book to acquaint yourself with the sewing machine and the techniques and supplies you'll need to get started. Your sewing machine owner's manual is a necessity; refer to it first if you have questions or problems specific to your machine.

Step one of any quilting project is to read the directions thoroughly. Refer to the "Tell Me More" sidebars for definitions or elaborations on any words or phrases printed in bold on the page. If the word or phrase is followed by a page number, its reference can be found on the page indicated. At the beginning of every project you will find a list telling you what you will need. Read through the information on fabrics before you go shopping so the fabric store will seem a little more user-friendly when you get there. Above all, have fun with these quilting projects, and enjoy the creative process while you learn new skills.

QUILTING BASICS

This book is written for the beginning quilter, but not everyone starts from the same place. Some beginners have sewing skills but have never sewn a quilt. Others have never sewn a stitch but quilting is where they want to begin. For someone new to quilting, even a trip to the quilt shop or fabric store can be challenging. Manufacturers can't include all the vital information with their packaging, and there are so many tools and quilting notions to choose from. To give you a firm foundation for learning to quilt, this section teaches you the essentials about your sewing machine, fabrics, sewing and quilting supplies, and specific quilting techniques. If you have never taken a stitch, you will appreciate the detailed information, photos, and illustrations. Even if you have sewing or quilting experience, you are sure to learn some things you didn't know. So settle back, take your time, and jump into the basics.

the sewing machine

The principle parts common to all sewing machines are shown and listed at right. The parts may look different on your model, and they may have slightly different locations, so open your owner's manual also. If you do not have an owner's manual for your machine, you should be able to get one from a sewing machine dealer who sells your brand or find one on the Internet. Become familiar with the names of the parts and their functions. As you spend more time sewing, these items will become second nature to you.

If you are buying a new machine, consider how much and what kind of sewing you expect to do. Talk to friends who sew and to sales personnel. Ask for demonstrations, and sew on the machine yourself. Experiment with the various features while sewing on a variety of fabrics, including knits, wovens, lightweights, and denim. Think about the optional features of the machine and which ones you want on yours. Leading sewing machine manufacturers offer a variety of models, including some that are specifically designed for machine quilting. You can, of course, do other kinds of sewing on these machines but they may have special features like a deeper bed to accommodate bulky layers for quilting, specialized feed systems, special presser feet for sewing accurate seams, and automatic stitch regulators to ensure even quilting stitches. Many dealers offer free sewing lessons with the purchase of a machine. Take advantage! These lessons will be geared to your particular brand and model of sewing machine.

These parts are common to all sewing machines, but their position and design differs. Use your manual to help you learn where these parts are, what these parts do, and how to use them:

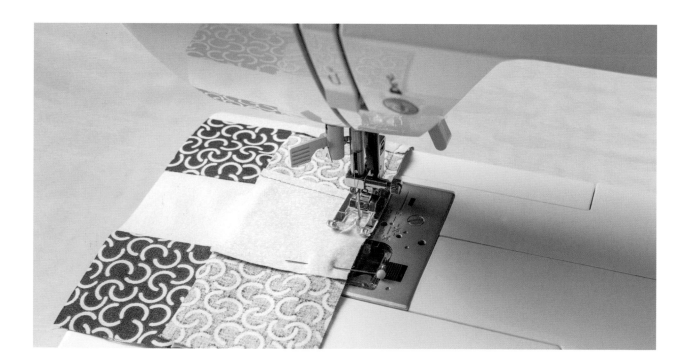

Bobbin

Bobbin case

Bobbin winder spindle

Bobbin winder tension

Buttonhole knob

Detachable machine bed

Feed dogs

Feed dog control

General-purpose presser foot

Handwheel

Light switch

Needle clamp

Presser foot lifter

Presser foot pressure control

Seam allowance guide

Spool pins

Stitch pattern selector

Stitch length selector

Stitch width selector

Take-up lever

Top tension control

Top tension discs

Thread cutter

Thread guides

Throat plate

Variable speed switch

machine accessories

SEWING MACHINE NEEDLES

Sewing machine needles come in a variety of styles and sizes. The correct needle choice depends mostly on the fabric you have selected. Sharp points (A), used for woven fabrics, are designed to pierce the fabric. Ballpoints (B) are designed to slip between the loops of knit fabric rather than pierce and possibly damage the fabric. Universal points are designed to work on both woven and knitted fabrics. The size of the needle is designated by a number, generally given in both American (9, 11, 12, 14, 16, 18) and European (60, 70, 80, 90, 100, 110) numbering systems. Use size 11/70 or 12/80 needles for mediumweight fabrics. A larger number means the needle is thicker and that it is appropriate for use with heavier fabrics and heavier threads.

A

B

TIP *Though needle style and size are usually indicated in some way on the needle, it is often difficult to see without a magnifying glass, and you most likely will not remember what needle is in the machine. As an easy reminder, when you finish a sewing session, leave a fabric swatch from your current project under the presser foot.*

BOBBINS

Stitches are made by locking the upper thread with a lower thread, carried on a bobbin. Always use bobbins in the correct style and size for your machine. Bobbin thread tension is controlled by a spring on the bobbin case, which may be built in (C) or removable (D).

C

D

PRESSER FEET

Every sewing machine comes with accessories for specialized tasks. More can be purchased as you develop your interest and skills. Your machine manual or dealer can show you what accessories are available and will explain how to use them to get the best results.

A general-purpose foot (A), probably the one you will use most often, has a wide opening to accommodate the side-to-side movement of the needle in all types of utility (nondecorative) stitches. It is also suitable for most straight stitching. A quarter-inch presser foot (B) aligns to the edge of the fabric to sew perfect ¼" (6 mm) seams, just right for piecing quilt blocks. A special-purpose or embroidery foot (C) has a grooved bottom that allows the foot to ride smoothly over decorative stitches or raised cords. Some styles have a wide space between the toes; others are clear plastic, allowing you to see your work more clearly. A walking foot (D) feeds top and bottom layers at equal rates, allowing you to more easily match patterns or stitch bulky layers, as in quilted projects. A zipper foot (E) is used to insert zippers or to stitch any seam that has more bulk on one side than the other. For some sewing machines, the zipper foot is stationary, requiring you to move the needle position to the right or left. For other styles, the position of the zipper foot itself is adjustable.

getting ready to sew

Simple tasks of inserting the needle, winding the bobbin, and threading the machine have tremendous influence on the stitch quality and performance of your machine. Use this guide as a general reference, but refer to your owner's manual for instructions specific to your machine.

INSERTING THE NEEDLE

Loosen the needle clamp. After selecting the appropriate needle for your project (page 12), insert it into the machine as high as it will go. The grooved side of the needle faces forward if your bobbin gets inserted from the front or top; it faces to the left if your bobbin gets inserted on the left. Tighten the clamp securely.

WINDING THE BOBBIN

If the bobbin case is built in, the bobbin is wound in place with the machine fully threaded as if to sew (page 16).

Removable bobbins are wound on the top or side of the machine, with the machine threaded for bobbin winding, as described in your owner's manual.

Bobbin thread must be drawn through the bobbin case tension spring. For wind-in-place bobbins, this happens automatically when you wind the bobbin, but you must do it manually when you insert a bobbin that already has thread on it.

After inserting the bobbin and threading the machine, you need to draw the bobbin thread to the top. Hold the needle thread while turning the handwheel toward you one full turn. As the needle goes down, the top thread interlocks with the bobbin thread and brings it up through the needle hole. Pull both threads together under the presser foot and off to the side or back.

THREADING THE MACHINE

Because every sewing machine is different, the threading procedure for your machine may differ slightly from the one shown here. Once again, it is important to refer to your owner's manual. Every upper thread guide adds a little tension to the thread as it winds its way to the needle. Missing one of them can make a big difference in the quality of your stitches.

1 Set the thread spool on the spindle. For a vertical spindle, position the spool so that it will turn clockwise as you sew. If the spindle is horizontal, the spool is held in place with an end cap. If your spool has a small cut in one end for minding the thread, position the spool with that end to the right.

TIP *If the spool is new and has paper labels covering the holes, poke them in, completely uncovering the holes, to allow the spool to turn freely.*

Unless your machine has a self-winding bobbin, you will want to wind the bobbin (page 14) before threading the machine.

2 Pull thread to the left and through the first thread guide

3 Draw thread through the tension guide.

TIP *It is very important to have the presser foot lever up when threading the machine because the tension discs are then open. If the presser foot is down and the discs are closed, the thread will not slide between the discs, and your stitches will not form correctly.*

4 Draw thread through the next thread guide.

5 Insert thread through the take-up lever.

6 Draw the thread through the remaining thread guides.

7 Thread the needle. Most needles are threaded from front to back; some from left to right.

1 Spool spindle

2 Thread guide

5 Take-up lever

3 Tension guide

4 Thread guide

6 Thread guide

7 Needle

how to balance tension

Your machine forms stitches by interlocking the bobbin thread with the needle thread. Every time the needle goes down into the fabric, a sharp hook catches the needle thread and wraps the bobbin thread around it. Imagine this little tug-of-war. If the needle thread tension is "stronger" than the bobbin thread tension, the needle thread pulls the bobbin thread through to the top. If the bobbin thread tension is "stronger," it pulls the needle thread through to the bottom. When the tensions are evenly balanced, the stitch will lock exactly halfway between the top and bottom of the layers being sewn, which is right where you want it.

Some machines have "self-adjusting tension," meaning the machine automatically adjusts its tension with every fabric you sew. For machines that do not have this feature, you may have to adjust the needle thread tension slightly as you sew different fabrics.

TESTING THE TENSION

1. Thread your machine and insert the bobbin, using two very different colors of thread, neither of which matches the fabric. Cut an 8" (20.5 cm) square of a smooth, mediumweight fabric. Fold the fabric in half diagonally, and place it under the presser foot so the fold aligns to your ½" (1.3 cm) seam guide. Lower the presser foot and set your stitch length at ten stitches per inch or 2.5 mm long.

2 Stitch a line across the fabric, stitching ½" (1.3 cm) from the diagonal fold. Remove the fabric from the machine. Inspect your stitching line from both sides. If your tension is evenly balanced, you will see only one color on each side. If you see both thread colors on the top side of your sample, the needle tension is tighter than the bobbin tension. If you see both thread colors on the back side of your sample, the bobbin tension is tighter than the needle tension.

3 Pull on your stitching line until you hear threads break. Because you stitched on the bias (page 26), the fabric will stretch slightly. If the thread breaks on only one side, your machine's tension is tighter on that side.

Top tension too tight

Top tension too loose

Tensions even

ADJUSTING THE TENSION

Before adjusting the tension on your machine, first check:

- that your machine is properly threaded (page 16)
- that your bobbin is properly installed
- that your needle is not damaged and is inserted correctly

After checking these three things, you may need to adjust the tension on your machine. (Check your owner's manual.) Tighten or loosen the needle thread tension slightly to bring the needle thread and bobbin thread tensions into balance. Test the stitches after each adjustment, until you achieve balanced tension. If slight adjustments of the needle tension dial do not solve the problem, the bobbin tension may need adjusting. However, most manufacturers do not recommend that you adjust bobbin tension yourself, so unless you have received instructions for adjusting the bobbin tension on your machine, take your machine in for repair.

quilt seams

Quilting is like putting puzzles together. Lots of squares, rectangles, triangles, and fabric strips are pieced together to make a colorful fabric picture. Every seam is sewn using ¼" (6 mm) seam allowances. In order to make all the pieces fit precisely, you must sew every seam accurately. Most machines have a seam allowance guide on the throat plate; however, it may not include a mark for ¼" (6 mm). For some presser feet, the distance from the needle tip to the edge of the foot is exactly ¼" (6 mm). If neither of these guides works for your machine, mark a ¼" (6 mm) seam guide on the bed of your machine with tape, as shown.

SEWING SEAMS

1 Thread your machine (page 16) and insert the bobbin (page 15). Holding the needle thread with your left hand, turn the handwheel toward you until the needle has gone down and come back up to its highest point. A stitch will form, and you will feel a tug on the needle thread. Pull on the needle thread to bring the bobbin thread up through the hole in the throat plate. Pull both threads together under the presser foot and off to one side.

2 Place two fabric squares right sides together, aligning the outer edges. Pin the pieces together along one long edge, inserting the pins perpendicular to the edge. Place the fabric under the presser foot so the pinned side edges align to the ¼" (6 mm) seam guide and the upper edges align to the needle hole in the throat plate. Lower the presser foot, and set your stitch length at 2 mm, which equals 15 stitches per inch.

3 Begin stitching slowly. Hold the thread tails under a finger for the first few stitches. This prevents the needle thread from being pulled out of the needle and also prevents the thread tails from being drawn down into the bobbin case, where they could cause a thread jam. Gently guide the fabric by walking your fingers ahead of and slightly to the sides of the presser foot. Remember, you are only guiding; let the machine pull the fabric.

TIP *Straight stitching lines are easier to achieve if you watch the edge of the fabric along the seam guide and ignore the needle. Sew smoothly at a relaxing pace, with minimal starting and stopping and without bursts of speed. You have better control of the speed if you operate your foot control with your heel resting on the floor.*

4 Stop stitching and remove pins as you come to them. When you reach the end of the fabric, stop again. Turn the handwheel toward you until the needle is in its highest position.

5 Raise the presser foot. Pull the fabric smoothly away from the presser foot, either to the left side or straight back. If you have to tug the threads, turn your handwheel slightly toward you until they pull easily. Cut the threads, leaving tails on the fabric and coming from the machine.

quilting supplies

The process of quilting involves several basic tasks: measuring, cutting, marking, and stitching. For each of these steps there are special tools and supplies to save you time, improve your accuracy, and make the project go smoothly.

MEASURING & CUTTING TOOLS

Buy quality cutting tools and use them only for sewing! Cutting paper and other non-fabric materials will dull your tools quickly. Sharp tools make precise cuts easier and, in the long run, will save you time.

Rotary cutters (A) allow you to cut smooth edges on multiple layers of fabric quickly and easily. The cutters are available in different sizes. Small cutters work well for curves and a few layers of fabric; the larger ones are ideal for long straight lines and many layers of fabric.

Cutting mats (B), made especially for use with rotary cutters, protect your blade and table top. Mats come in a variety of sizes. Choose one at least 22" (56 cm) wide to accommodate a width of fabric folded in half. A mat with a printed grid is a useful guide for cutting right angles.

You'll want a clear quilting ruler (C) to use as a measuring tool and as a guide for your rotary cutter. A ruler 6" × 24" (15 × 61 cm) is a popular, versatile size. Square rulers and rulers with 30°, 45°, and 60° angle lines also are available.

Sewing scissors (D) and shears (E) are sewing necessities. Purchase the best quality you can afford.

MARKING TOOLS

The marks you make on fabric should last only as long as you need them. You should be able to remove them easily without damaging the quilt.

Always test a marker on a sample swatch of fabric first and remember to mark lightly!

A special fabric eraser (F) can be used to remove light lead pencil marks without damaging fabric. Quilter's pencils (G), available in white or gray lead, have eraser ends for easy removal. The leads are oil-free and contain less graphite to prevent smearing. Soapstone pencils (H), made of pressed talc, can be sharpened to a fine point and rubbed off or wiped with a damp cloth. Water-soluble pencils (I), handy for marking on darker fabrics, can be removed with a damp cloth.

PINS, NEEDLES & THREAD

Quilting pins (A), used for pinning your pieces together, are 1¾" (4.5 cm) long and have large glass heads.

Curved, rustproof safety pins (B) in 1" to 1½" (2.5 to 3.8 cm) size make quick work of basting your quilting projects.

Milliner's needles (C) with small, round eyes are preferred by quilters who want to hand-baste the layers together.

Betweens (D) are short needles with round eyes for sewing small hand-quilting stitches.

Sharps, similar to betweens but slightly longer, are used for appliquéing and general hand sewing.

Cotton-covered polyester threads and 100% cotton threads (E) are available for machine and hand quilting. Hand-quilting threads have a polished glacé finish that provides abrasion resistance and prevents tangling and knotting; 100% cotton basting thread is also available.

Fine monofilament thread (F) can also be used for machine quilting, making the stitches less noticeable.

PRESSING EQUIPMENT & TECHNIQUES

Pressing at each stage of construction is the secret to perfect piecing. The general rule is to press each stitched seam before crossing it with another. Often you can sew the same seam in numerous sets before making the trip to the ironing board to press them all.

Pressing your seams carefully is crucial to your success, second only to accurate sewing of the ¼" (6 mm) seams. Use the tip of the iron, moving only in the direction of the grainlines. Be especially cautious when pressing seams sewn on the bias. Careless pressing can distort the shape and size of your quilt project. Both seam allowances are usually pressed together to one side or the other. Following the pressing plan in the project directions will help you produce a neat, precise design.

Use a steam/spray iron with a wide temperature range. Buy a dependable, name-brand iron. Because your iron will be left on and standing still for several minutes between pressing steps, avoid an iron with an automatic shut-off feature.

An ironing board provides a sufficient surface for pressing, but you may want to invest in a foldout surface, such as the one, shown. It has a cotton cover printed with a measured grid to help you press your pieces more accurately.

fabric information

After you have chosen a quilt design, it's time to select the fabric. This may seem like a difficult task at first, but consider it an adventure and have fun. This is the time to use your vision and creativity. Just as two painters can paint the same landscape and produce very different effects, your choice of patterns, colors, and the way you combine them will give each project your unique style.

Fabrics made of 100% cotton or cotton blends can be used. Both are available in a wide variety of patterns and colors, so you'll have plenty of options to choose from. Many quilters prefer using 100% cotton fabrics because they find them easier to sew, press, mark, and hand-quilt.

If you are shopping for your fabrics in a quilt shop, they will probably be arranged according to their colors or print types, and you'll rarely find fabric that is not pure cotton. In a general fabric store, you may find a section for quilting fabrics, but there are probably other suitable fabrics located elsewhere in the store. Be sure to check the labels for fiber content and care.

The outer edges of woven fabrics are called selvages. As a general rule, they should be trimmed away (page 33), because they are more tightly woven than the rest of the fabric, and they may shrink when laundered or pressed. Grainlines are the directions in which the fabric yarns run. Strong, stable, lengthwise yarns, running parallel to the selvages, form the lengthwise grain. The crosswise grain is perpendicular to the lengthwise grain and has a small amount of give. The diagonal direction, which has considerable stretch, is called the bias.

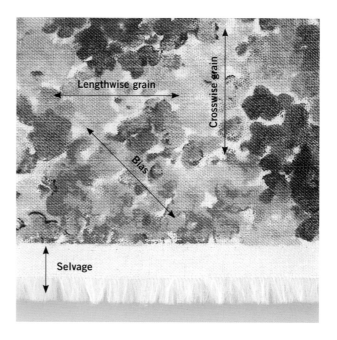

PRINTS

Printed cotton fabrics are available in a wide range of design styles and print sizes. They include batiks, plaids, florals, tiny-grained prints that "read" as solids, and soft flannels.

SOLIDS

Solid-color fabrics come in a rainbow of colors, with shades and tints to suit any purpose. They include a variety of hand-dyed cottons that have a subtle sueded look. You'll often find them in packets of graduated color values or hues. Muslin, available bleached or unbleached, is usually used for the background pieces in a design, for plain blocks, or for the quilt backing.

BACKING FABRICS

The backing fabric should have the same care requirements as the fabrics in the quilt top. For smaller projects, especially when the backing is visible, back the quilt top with one of the fabrics used on the front. For wall hangings and other items where the backing is rarely seen, muslin is a good choice. If you want to accentuate the quilting stitches on the backing side, choose a solid-colored fabric. Printed fabrics tend to hide the stitches.

PREPARING THE FABRIC

Preshrink your fabric, especially if you intend to launder the finished project. Most cotton fabrics shrink 2 to 3 percent when washed and dried, so if they're not preshrunk, the fabrics may pucker at the stitching lines and the finished size of the quilted piece may change the first time it is washed.

Launder fabrics in your washing machine on a short, warm cycle. There's no need to use detergent, but be sure to wash like colors together in case they aren't colorfast. Check the rinse water of dark or vivid fabrics to be sure they are colorfast; if dye transfers to the water, continue rinsing the fabric until the water is clear. Machine dry the fabric until it is only slightly damp, and then press it.

SELECTING FABRICS

Use contrasting colors to make the pieces of a quilt block stand out from each other. Combine warm colors (reds, yellows, or oranges) in the same quilt block with cool colors (blues, greens, or violets) to make them all seem more vivid, as shown in the Log Cabin block (at right).

Any fabric shape, whether solid-color or print, will "pop" from the quilt surface when surrounded by white or nearly white fabric. This is readily apparent in the placemat (below, left).

Select a multicolor print first, perhaps for the border. Then select fabrics for the quilt block pieces, drawing colors from the print, as shown in the Star Sashing quilt (below, right).

Interesting visual effects are achieved by using colors with graduated values (lightness or darkness). Stack all the fabrics you are considering on a table; then stand back and squint. Or view them through a special filtering tool, available at quilt shops, designed for judging color values. The filter blocks out color and reveals only the lightness or darkness of the fabric.

Combine fabrics with various print scales and styles to add visual texture to your quilt. Don't be afraid to cut up a large-scale print into smaller pieces.

selecting the batting

The middle layer of the quilt is called the batting. When selecting batting for any project, consider the amount of loft, its drapability, and the distance required between quilting stitches to prevent the batting from bunching or pulling apart. This distance, usually ranging from 1" to 6" (2.5 to 15 cm), is printed on the package label.

Cotton, polyester, and cotton/polyester blends are the most common fibers used in batting. Cotton batting gives a flat, traditional appearance when quilted. It absorbs moisture and is cool in the summer and warm in the winter. Polyester batting is more durable, is easier to handle than cotton, and gives a slightly puffier look. It provides warmth without weight, is nonallergenic, and resists moth and mildew damage. For the traditional appearance of cotton, but the stability and ease in handling of polyester, choose a cotton/polyester blend.

Low-loft battings are recommended for machine quilting but even low-loft battings vary in thickness. Extra-low-loft battings are often used for garments or placemats. For wall hangings or lap quilts, select a low-loft batting that is sturdy but drapable.

Batting is available in a wide range of sizes, although the selection in certain fibers and construction types may be limited. Available in quilting stores and many fabric stores, batting can be purchased by the yard and in small packages for clothing and craft projects. It is also packaged for standard-size bed quilts.

(Above Left) Low-loft polyester batting, used in this wall hanging, is easy to machine-quilt and very durable.

(Above Right) Cotton/polyester low-loft batting provides warmth, durability, and easy laundering for a child's quilt.

(Left) Extra-low-loft polyester batting is a good choice for placemats or table runners, when you want a subtle quilted look for an item that may be laundered often.

rotary cutting

Accuracy in cutting is critical to successful quilting. A small error, multiplied by each piece, will result in blocks that don't fit together. You don't need that kind of frustration when you are learning to quilt! Take the time to cut accurately, and give yourself a head start in the quilting game.

You'll find the investment in a rotary cutter and mat well worth it, once you start to use them. While indispensable for quilting, they are also perfectly suited for many other sewing projects. Rotary cutting is not only a very accurate method, it also saves time. Instead of cutting each piece of the quilt individually, you can cut several identical pieces at once and have the entire project cut and ready to sew in minutes.

TIP *Because rotary cutters are extremely sharp, the manufacturers have designed ways to cover or retract the blades. Always use this safety feature every time you put the tool down. An open blade falling from a table can easily slice through leather shoes. Keep your fingers out of the way when you are cutting, avoiding awkward positions where you have less control. Above all, keep the cutters in a safe place where children will not find them.*

STRAIGHTENING THE FABRIC

1 First, determine the grainline. Fold the fabric in half and hold it by the selvages. Shift the edges, if necessary, until the fabric hangs straight. The foldline is the straight lengthwise grain.

2 Lay the fabric on the cutting mat, with the fold along a grid line. Place the ruler on the fabric, close to the raw edge, at a 90° angle to the fold. Holding the ruler firmly in place with one hand, trim the excess fabric off along the edge of the ruler, using the rotary cutter. Apply steady, firm pressure to the blade. Stop when the rotary cutter gets past your hand.

3 Leave the blade in position, and reposition your hand on the ruler ahead of the blade. Hold firmly, and continue cutting. Make sure the fabric and the ruler don't move. Shift your hand position on the ruler whenever necessary.

4 Reposition the folded fabric on the cutting mat with the straightened end on a horizontal grid line. Place the ruler over the fabric perpendicular to the cut end, with the edge just inside the selvages. Cut off the selvages, using the rotary cutter as in steps 2 and 3.

CUTTING STRIPS

1 Position the folded fabric so that the edge you will be cutting is on the left if you are right-handed, or on the right if you are left-handed. Place the ruler on the fabric, aligning the trimmed edge with the appropriate measurement on the ruler. Holding the ruler firmly, cut as on page 33, steps 2 and 3.

2 Lift the ruler and move the cut strip so that you are able to see the cutting line. Reposition the ruler and cut the next strip.

TIP *These photos show you how a right-handed person would hold the ruler and rotary cutter. If you are left-handed, you would hold the tools in opposite hands and work from the opposite direction.*

CUTTING SQUARES OR RECTANGLES

1 Stack three or four strips, matching the edges exactly. Place the ruler on the fabric, aligning the short edge of the fabric with the appropriate measurement on the ruler. Hold the ruler firmly in place. Cut the fabric, guiding the rotary cutter along the edge of the ruler.

CUTTING TRIANGLES

1 Stack three or four squares, matching the edges exactly. Place the ruler over the squares diagonally, aligning it exactly to the corners of the squares. Cut through the squares, guiding the rotary cutter along the edge of the ruler. The project directions will tell you what size to cut the squares and whether to cut them diagonally once or twice.

CUTTING A RECTANGLE WIDER THAN THE RULER

1 Measure the width of the strip in from the cut edge in several places; mark the fabric, using chalk or a pencil.

2 Align the ruler to the marks, and hold it firmly in place. Cut the fabric, guiding the rotary cutter along the edge of the ruler over the marks.

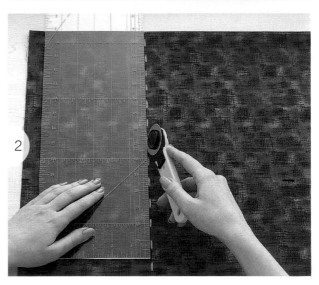

layering and basting

Every quilt project, from the simplest one-piece hot pad to a multi-block bed quilt, must be layered and basted before you proceed with the actual quilting stitches. Basting keeps the quilt top, batting, and backing from shifting while you are quilting.

Traditionally, quilts have been basted using a hand needle and thread. While this is still a viable alternative, you may save a little time basting with safety pins. If you prefer basting with thread, use a single strand of white cotton thread and a large milliner's or darning needle. For safety-pin basting, use only rustproof pins in either 1" or 1½" (2.5 or 3.8 cm) size. Special quilter's safety pins are bent for easier insertion. For either method, follow the same steps for layering the quilt.

LAYERING THE QUILT

1 Press the quilt top and backing fabric flat. Mark the center of each side of the quilt top at the raw edges, using safety pins. Repeat this step for the batting and the backing. Place the backing on your work surface, wrong side up. Use masking tape to tape the backing securely to your work surface, beginning at the center of each side and working toward the corners. Keep the fabric taut but not stretched.

2 Place the batting on the backing, matching the center pins on all sides. Smooth the batting (but don't stretch it), working from the center of the quilt out to the sides.

3 Place the quilt top, right side up, over the batting, matching the pins on each side. Again, smooth the fabric without stretching it. For clarity, the photos show a solid piece of fabric in place of a multicolor pieced quilt top.

BASTING WITH THREAD

1 Thread the needle with a long strand of thread; tie a knot in the end. Begin at the center of the quilt, and stitch toward the side, taking 1" (2.5 cm) stitches through all three layers. Avoid stitching directly on seamlines or marked quilting lines. Pull the stitches snug so the layers will not shift.

2 Baste to the side of the quilt. **Backstitch** two or three stitches to secure.

3 Repeat steps 1 and 2 in each direction, so that you have divided the quilt into four quadrants with the basting stitches.

TIP *As you run out of thread, backstitch a few stitches. Then rethread the needle, knot the thread, and continue basting from where you stopped.*

tell me more

BACKSTITCH. Take a few stitches in the opposite direction when you get to the end of a basting row. This will hold the basting in place but is easier to remove than a knot.

4 Baste parallel rows of stitches, no less than 6" (15 cm) apart, in one quadrant of the quilt. Work from the existing basting line toward the outer edge. Then repeat with parallel rows in the opposite direction.

5 Repeat step 4 for each quadrant of the quilt. Remove the tape from the backing. Fold the edges of the backing over the batting and edges of the quilt top, and safety-pin them in place. This prevents the raw edges from raveling and prevents the batting from catching on the needle and feed dogs during quilting.

BASTING WITH SAFETY PINS

Follow the same guidelines, first dividing the quilt into quadrants, and then working on one quadrant at a time. Insert all the pins in the same direction. Space them no more than 6" (15 cm) apart in parallel rows, vertically and horizontally. Avoid placing pins where you will be quilting.

TIP *Safety-pin basting goes more quickly if the pins are all open. In fact, they can be purchased at quilting stores already opened. Then, as you remove them from your quilt, leave them open and ready for the next project. You'll save a little wear and tear on your fingers.*

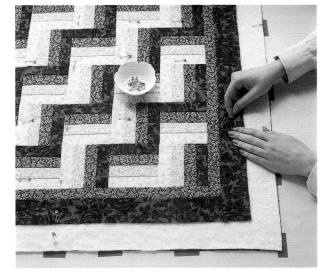

basic quilting techniques

Quilting stitches hold the quilt top, batting, and backing of the quilt together. But beyond its function, quilting adds texture and interest to the quilt, enhancing its pieced design. For best effect, the quilting should reinforce or complement the piecing or appliqué design, and it should form an appealing design on the back as well as the front of the quilt.

You can quilt by hand or by machine; there are advantages to either method. Hand quilting is the traditional method, and many quilters still prefer it that way. Machine quilting, of course, takes less time and is also more durable. Whether quilting by hand or machine, your stitching should cover the surface of the quilt uniformly. This guideline is more than just an aesthetic consideration; heavily quilted areas tend to shrink more than lightly quilted areas.

MATERIALS

FOR HAND QUILTING
- Hand-quilting thread
- Between or sharp hand needle (page 24)
- Thimble
- Quilting hoop

FOR MACHINE QUILTING
- Walking foot

HAND QUILTING

1 Center the area you will work on in your quilting hoop. Thread a between or sharp needle with a single strand of hand-quilting thread, about 18" (46 cm) long; tie a small knot in the end. Take one long stitch, inserting the needle from the front into the batting, about 1" (2.5 cm) from where you want to begin stitching. Don't stitch through to the backing. Bring the needle up where you will begin quilting.

2 Pull on your thread, gently "popping" the knot under the surface of the fabric. Don't pull too hard, or you'll pull the stitch out completely.

3 Take small, even stitches, up and down, through all three layers. If possible, take two to four stitches on your needle before pulling it through the quilt. Strive for quilting that looks the same on the front and the back of the quilt. The stitches should be the same length on both sides.

TIP *To avoid poking a hole in the finger that pushes the needle, you'll want to wear a thimble. Many quilters find leather thimbles more comfortable than plastic or metal.*

4 To finish a row of quilting, tie a small knot close to the surface of the fabric next to your last stitch. Use your thumbnail to gently pull the fabric, again "popping" the knot under the surface of the fabric. Take a shallow stitch, and clip the thread.

TIP *While small stitches are desirable, uniformity is more important. Practice taking six stitches per inch (2.5 cm) as a beginner.*

MACHINE QUILTING

1 Attach a walking foot (page 13). Place the quilt under the foot, in the area where you will begin quilting. Lower the foot. Turn the handwheel by hand for one stitch, and stop with the needle at the highest position. Raise the foot, and pull on the needle thread to bring the bobbin thread up through the fabric.

2 Draw both threads under the walking foot to one side. Lower the walking foot, with the needle aligned to enter the fabric at the desired starting point.

3 Stitch several very short stitches to secure the threads at the beginning of the stitching line. Gradually increase the stitch length for about ½" (1.3 cm), until it is the desired length; about 15 stitches per inch, which equals 2 mm.

4 Slow your stitching as you approach a stopping point. Beginning about ½" (1.3 cm) from the end, gradually decrease the stitch length until you are barely moving, to secure the threads.

TIP *Stitch with your hands positioned on either side of the walking foot, holding the fabric taut.*

MACHINE-QUILTING PATTERNS

A Stitch-in-the-ditch quilting emphasizes the pieced design because it is stitched following the seamlines for the blocks. Stitch so that the needle enters the well of the seam.

B Channel quilting is stitched in relatively evenly spaced lines. You can mark them before you layer and baste the quilt or, for a less formal look, you can stitch them more irregularly. The quilting lines can be diagonal, vertical, or horizontal.

C Outline quilting. Stitch about ¼" (6 mm) away from the seamlines.

TIP *Whenever you need to change direction, stop with the needle down in the fabric. Raise the walking foot, and pivot. Then lower the walking foot and continue stitching.*

binding

Binding is the final step for most of your quilting projects. Enclosing the edges of the quilt, the binding forms a clean, attractive finish. Binding fabrics can either match or complement the other fabrics in the quilt. Very often a quilt is bound in the same fabric as the outer border.

BINDING A QUILT

1 Cut 3" (7.5 cm) binding strips from the entire crosswise width of the fabric. If the sides of your quilt are shorter than the length of the binding strips, go on to step 3. If the sides of your quilt are longer than one binding strip, pin two strips, right sides together, at right angles. Mark a diagonal line from the corner of the upper strip to the corner of the lower strip. Stitch on the marked line.

2 Trim the seam allowances to ¼" (6 mm). Press the seam open.

3 Press the binding strips in half lengthwise, wrong sides together.

4 Measure the quilt top across the middle, from side to side. Cut two binding strips equal to this measurement plus 2" (5 cm). Mark the binding strips 1" (2.5 cm) from the ends. Divide the length between the pins in fourths, and pin-mark. Also divide the upper and lower edges of the quilt in fourths, and pin-mark.

 tell me more

MEASURE THE QUILT TOP ACROSS THE MIDDLE. After piecing and quilting a quilt top, it is likely that the top and bottom may be slightly different lengths. By making both bindings the same length as the middle of the quilt, you are able to square up the finished project.

(continued)

5 Pin a binding strip on the right side of the upper edge of the quilt, aligning the raw edges of the binding to the raw edge of the quilt top and matching the pin marks. **Insert the pins perpendicular to the raw edges.** The binding will extend 1" (2.5 cm) beyond the quilt at each end.

6 Stitch the binding strip to the quilt ¼" (6 mm) from the raw edges of the binding. **Remove the pins as you come to them.**

7 Trim off the excess batting and backing ½" (1.3 cm) from the stitching line.

8 Wrap the binding snugly around the edge of the quilt, covering the stitching line on the back of the quilt. Pin the binding in place from the right side, inserting the pins parallel to the binding in the seam "ditch" and catching the folded edge on the back. For easy removal, insert all the pins so that the heads will be toward you when you are stitching.

 tell me more

INSERT THE PINS PERPENDICULAR TO THE RAW EDGES. This makes it easier to remove them as you sew. The pin heads are near the raw edge where you can grasp them with your right hand. In this position, you are much less likely to stick yourself with a pin as you sew.

REMOVE PINS AS YOU COME TO THEM. As tempting as it may be, don't sew over pins! You may be lucky and save a few seconds, or you could hit a pin and break your needle, costing you much more time in the long run.

9 Stitch in the ditch (page 43) on the right side of the quilt, catching the binding on the back of the quilt. Remove the pins as you come to them.

10 Repeat steps 5 to 9 for the lower edge of the quilt. Trim the ends of the upper and lower binding strips even with the edges of the quilt top.

11 Repeat steps 4 to 7 for the sides of the quilt, measuring the quilt top down the middle, from top to bottom, in step 4. Trim the ends of the binding strips to extend ½" (1.3 cm) beyond the finished edges of the quilt.

12 Wrap and pin the binding around the edge, as in step 8. At each end, fold in the raw edges of the binding. Then fold under the ½" (1.3 cm) end; press. Finish wrapping and pinning the binding. Stitch the binding as in step 9.

QUILTING PROJECTS

IIVIIVIIVIIIIIIIIIIIIIIIIIIIIIIVIIVIIVIIVIII/IIIIIIIIIIIIIIIIIIVIIVIIVIIVII

The eleven projects in this section are loosely arranged in order of difficulty, and different quilting techniques are taught in each project. They include useful items like coasters, placemats, and hot pads; decorative items like wall quilts; and quilts used for warmth. While you probably will not make all the projects in order, it is worth your time to at least read through all the projects and study the techniques introduced in each one.

RAW-EDGE APPLIQUÉ HOT PAD

Raw-edge appliqués add dimension and interest to a quilted project. Practice the technique by creating a set of hot pads. Because the batting is quite thin, these hot pads are more decorative than useful. For the appliqués, draw patterns freehand or find simple clip art shapes. Because the edges will not be finished in any way, avoid any long narrow extensions or small details that could ravel away entirely. The edges of the appliqués can be frayed with a stiff brush. For minimal fraying, use a tightly woven fabric for the appliqué. If you would like a more natural frayed look, machine wash and tumble dry the hot pads. The finished hot pad is about 9" (23 cm) square.

MATERIALS

- ⅜ yd. (0.35 m) background fabric, for the hot pad
- ¼ yd. (0.25 m) contrasting fabric, for the appliqué and binding
- Low-loft batting, about 13" (33 cm) square
- Rotary cutter and mat
- Quilting ruler
- Thread to match or blend with the fabrics
- Glue stick
- Decorative ring

SKILLS

- Raw-edge appliqué
- Channel quilting

HOW TO SEW A RAW-EDGE APPLIQUÉ HOT PAD

1 Straighten the cut ends of the fabric, and trim off the selvages (page 33). Cut a 9" (23 cm) square of background fabric for the hot pad front. Cut a 13" (33 cm) square of background fabric for the back. Cut a 13" (33 cm) square of batting. Cut four 3" × 11" (7.5 × 28 cm) strips of contrasting fabric for the binding. Cut an appliqué from the contrasting fabric, about 6" (15 cm) wide.

2 **Glue-baste** the appliqué, right side up, to the right side of the hot pad front. Position the appliqué as desired in the center of the square.

3 Layer and baste the hot pad (page 36). Remove the layers from the work surface. Attach a walking foot (page 13), if you have one. Set your stitch length at 12 stitches per inch, which equals 2.5 mm. Begin stitching in the upper right corner of the pad, about 1" (2.5 cm) from the cut edge of the top layer.

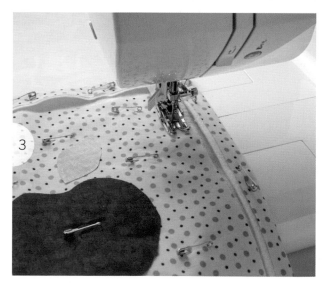

4 Stitch from top to bottom, **stopping with the needle down in the fabric.** Lift the presser foot, pivot the hot pad 90°, and lower the presser foot. Stitch about 1" (2.5 cm). Stopping with the needle down, lift the presser foot, and pivot the hot pad another 90° to begin a new row of stitching.

5 Repeat this process until the entire hot pad is channel-quilted (page 43), catching the appliqué in the stitching. If you basted the hot pad with safety pins, remove them as you come to them.

6 Bind the edges of the hot pad, following the directions on page 44. Hand-stitch a small decorative ring to one corner, for hanging, if desired.

TIP *Relax! The rows of channel quilting don't need to be perfectly parallel. In fact, some variation is desirable to give it handmade charm.*

tell me more

GLUE-BASTE. Using a fabric glue stick, apply dots of glue to the wrong side of the appliqué. This will hold it temporarily in place until you catch it permanently to the hot pad with quilting stitches.

STOPPING WITH THE NEEDLE DOWN IN THE FABRIC. Stop running the machine with the foot pedal. Turn the handwheel on your machine manually until the needle is all the way down into the fabric.

PAPER-PIECED LOG CABIN COASTERS

This festive coaster set introduces you to the popular quilting technique of paper piecing or foundation piecing. Fabric pieces are roughly cut for each numbered section of a paper pattern. Translucent foundation paper, available at quilt shops, works very well because you can see through it without having to hold it to a light source. With fabrics aligned on the underside of the pattern, the pieces are stitched together through the lines on the paper, one piece at a time in a numbered sequence. Seam allowances are trimmed down after each stitching line, eliminating the need for precise cutting of the design pieces beforehand. Each design goes together in minutes, and it's nearly impossible to make a mistake!

MATERIALS

○ Translucent foundation paper

○ Pattern (page 61)

○ #2 pencil or fine-point permanent marker

○ Small straightedge

○ Small scraps of various fabrics in small-grain prints and solid colors, as suggested in the photo

○ ¼ yd. (0.25 m) extra-low-loft batting

○ ¼ yd. (0.25 m) fabric for borders and lining

○ Temporary fabric adhesive

○ Hand needle and thread

SKILLS

○ Paper-piecing

○ Finger-pressing seam allowances

○ Lining to the edge

○ Slipstitching

HOW TO SEW A PAPER-PIECED COASTER

1 Trace the pattern on page 61 onto foundation paper, using a fine-point permanent marker or #2 pencil. Cut out the pattern, allowing a ½" (1.3 cm) margin around the outside. Number the design sections. The side with the lines is actually the pattern back. The fabrics will be sewn to the blank or front side. Cut a piece of fabric for each section of the design, making each piece about ¾" (2 cm) larger than the area it has to cover. The pieces can be square, rectangular, or irregular.

2 Place the pattern so the blank (right) side faces up. Center and pin the first fabric piece over section 1, with the right side of the fabric facing up. Pin in place, **inserting the pin where it won't interfere with stitching lines.** Check from the back (printed side) to see that the fabric extends at least ¼" (6 mm) beyond all the lines for section 1.

1

2

3 Place the second fabric piece over the first piece, right sides together, roughly aligning the raw edges between sections 1 and 2. Pin along the shared pattern line, with the pin inserted on the line.

4 Flip the second fabric piece over to confirm that the fabric extends at least ¼" (6 mm) beyond the section 2 lines. Adjust the position of the second piece, if necessary. Fold the second piece back, right sides together, over the first. Move the pin to a place away from the stitching line.

 tell me more

INSERTING THE PIN WHERE IT WON'T INTERFERE WITH STITCHING LINES. The pin will be on the underside as you stitch, and difficult to move out of the way. Place it where it won't be run over by the presser foot or hit by the needle. With some practice, you will be able to paper-piece without using pins at all.

3

4

(continued)

5 Set the machine for a **short straight stitch** of 12 to 15 stitches per inch or 2 mm. Place the pattern, printed side up, under the presser foot, with the needle aligned to the shared stitching line between sections 1 and 2. Lower the presser foot and begin stitching two or three stitch lengths before the line. Stitch on the line to the end and stitch two or three stitches beyond the end of the line. Raise the presser foot. Carefully remove the pattern and fabric from the machine, clipping the threads close to the pattern.

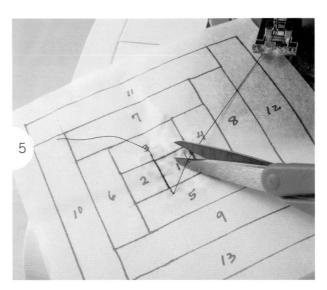

6 Remove the pins. Flip the pattern over and **trim the seam allowances down to about ¼" (6 mm) beyond the stitching line**. Finger-press the second fabric away from the first along the stitching line.

TIP *Finger-pressing saves time. Rather than running over to the ironing board after the addition of each piece, the fabrics are temporarily smoothed into place with your fingers. Place the pattern right side up on a flat surface. Flip the just-sewn piece over so the right side faces out. Run your fingernail over the seam to flatten it and extend the piece to its full size.*

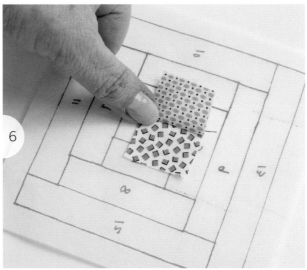

7 Place the third fabric piece over the second piece, right sides together. Pin along the shared pattern line, with the pin inserted on the line. Flip the third piece over to confirm that the fabric extends at least ¼" (6 mm) beyond the section 3 lines. Adjust the position of the third piece, if necessary. Fold the third piece back over the second. Repin the fabric in place away from the stitching line.

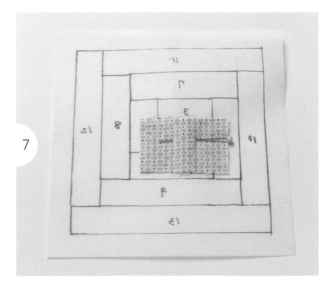

8 Stitch on the shared design line between sections 2 and 3, as in step 6. Trim the seam allowances and finger-press the third piece as in steps 7 and 8. Follow the same procedure, adding pieces in numbered sequence until the entire pattern is complete.

![sewing machine icon] *tell me more*

SHORT STRAIGHT STITCH. Stitches that are closer together will be more difficult to remove if you make a mistake, but they are also more secure and make it easier to tear away the paper after the design is sewn.

TRIM THE SEAM ALLOWANCES ¼" (6 MM) BEYOND THE STITCHING LINE. Fold the paper out of the way and trim off the excess fabric to within ¼" (6 mm) of the stitching line, using a scissors. The seam allowances do not have to be accurately cut.

9 Stitch around the entire pattern, just outside the outer design line. Press. Trim off the excess fabric ¼" (6 mm) beyond the stitching line. Carefully tear away the paper from the back of the design.

10 Cut a 5" (12.7 cm) square for the backing and a 5" (12.7 cm) square of the batting. Spray a light coat of temporary fabric adhesive to one side of the batting. Smooth the pieced coaster, right side up, over the batting. Place backing over the pieced top, right sides together. Pin the layers together, **inserting the pins perpendicular to the edges** (p. 46). Stitch ¼" (6 mm) seam all around, pivoting at the corners. Leave a 2" (5 cm) opening along the bottom edge for turning.

(continued)

11 Trim the batting close to the stitching. Trim the corners diagonally to reduce bulk.

12 Turn the coaster right side out through the opening; press. Using a hand needle and thread, slipstitch the opening closed, alternating small stitches from one side of the opening to the other as shown.

13 Attach a walking foot (page 13) and lengthen the stitch length slightly. Quilt the coaster by stitching in the ditch of the seam (page 43) between the outer border and the design.

NINE-PATCH PILLOW

This charming pillow is made by stitching nine squares of fabric together in a checkerboard pattern. You'll need to select two coordinating prints, a coordinating print and solid, or two contrasting solids. The checkerboard pattern is repeated on the back of the pillow, with the squares arranged in the reverse order. The front and back are pieced separately; then each is layered with batting and backing and quilted before sewing them together to make the pillow cover.

MATERIALS

- ½ yd. (0.5 m) each of two coordinating fabrics
- ⅝ yd. (0.6 m) muslin, for the pillow backing
- ⅝ yd. (0.6 m) batting
- Rotary cutter and mat
- Quilting ruler
- Thread to match or blend with the fabrics
- 18" (46 cm) square pillow form
- Hand needle

SKILLS

- Accurate cutting and piecing
- Matching seams perfectly
- Stitching in the ditch

HOW TO SEW A NINE-PATCH PILLOW

1 Straighten the cut ends of the fabrics, and trim off the selvages (page 33).

2 With the fabric still folded in half, cut two 6½" (16.5 cm) strips of fabric across the entire width, from the cut edges to the fold. Cut nine 6½" (16.5 cm) squares from these strips.

3 Repeat steps 1 and 2 for fabric B. Arrange the squares in two nine-patch blocks, as shown.

4 Pin one A square to one B square along one side, with right sides together, **inserting pins perpendicular to the edges** (p. 46). Align the cut ends and edges. Place the fabric under the presser foot, aligning the upper edges to the needle hole in the throat plate. Align the cut edges of the fabric to the ¼" (6 mm) seam allowance guide (page 20) on your machine. Stitch a ¼" (6 mm) seam, **removing pins as you come to them** (p. 46).

5 Pin another A square to the opposite side of the B square. Stitch a ¼" (6 mm) seam, forming a three-square strip.

6 Repeat steps 4 and 5 to make two more identical three-square strips. Then sew the remaining strips together, with an A square in the center of each. Press the seam allowances **toward the darker fabric**. The strips should now measure 6½" × 18½" (16.5 × 47 cm).

7 Beginning with the pillow front, pin the top strip to the center strip, with right sides together and raw edges even. Align the seams, **inserting the pins in the wells of the seams.** You will notice that the matching seam allowances turn in opposite directions. Stitch a ¼" (6 mm) seam, removing pins as you come to them.

TIP *To ensure smooth seams and perfect intersections, slow down as you approach each one. Stop with the needle down in the fabric, raise the presser foot, and lift the edges slightly from the machine bed. Make sure the seam allowances on the underside are still turned in the direction they were pressed. Then lower the presser foot and continue sewing.*

8 Pin the remaining strip to the opposite side of the center strip, pinning as in step 7; stitch the seam. You have just completed a nine-patch block. Press both seam allowances away from the center.

tell me more

TOWARD THE DARKER FABRIC. In piecing a quilt top, seam allowances are usually pressed toward darker pieces to avoid show-through under light-colored pieces.

INSERTING THE PINS IN THE WELLS OF THE SEAMS. By pinning in this manner, you are making sure that the stitched seams will line up perfectly on the right side. Stitch up to these pins as close as you can before removing them.

(continued)

9 Repeat steps 7 and 8 for the pillow back. Cut two squares of muslin and two squares of batting, each 4" (10 cm) larger than the pillow front and back. Layer and baste the front and back (page 36).

10 Remove the layers from the work surface. Set your stitch length at 10 to 12 stitches per inch, which equals 2.5 mm. Attach a walking foot (page 13), if you have one, or use an all-purpose presser foot. Quilt each block, using the stitch-in-the-ditch method (page 43) along all the seams.

11 Set your stitch length to long, and machine-baste around the pillow top a scant ¼" (6 mm) from the edge of the top fabric. Trim the batting and muslin even with the edges of the top fabric, using a rotary cutter and mat. Repeat for the pillow back.

12 Place the pillow back over the pillow front, with right sides together, matching the raw edges. Align the seams of the front block to the corresponding seams of the back block. Insert pins in the wells of the seams.

13 Stitch around the pillow cover, ¼" (6 mm) from the raw edges leaving a 10" (25.5 cm) opening along one side. Trim the corners diagonally, to remove excess bulk.

14 Turn the pillow cover right side out through the opening. Use a point turner or similar tool to carefully push the corners out, if necessary. Insert the pillow form into the pillow cover. Pin the opening closed. Slipstitch the opening closed, alternating small stitches from one side of the opening to the other as shown.

CHECKERBOARD PLACEMATS

Add homespun charm to your dining table with this set of four checkerboard placemats. Select two coordinating print fabrics, a print and a solid, or two solids, preferably with a high contrast between them.

The directions are for four placemats. You will find that this strip-piecing method of construction saves time in sewing and cuts down on the number of trips back and forth to the ironing board. Set your machine for a straight stitch of 10 to 12 stitches per inch, which equals 2.5 mm, and sew ¼" (6 mm) seam allowances throughout the entire project. Each placemat measures about 14" × 18" (35.5 × 46 cm).

MATERIALS

- ½ yd. (0.5 m) light-colored print or solid fabric, we'll call "A"

- 2 yd. (1.85 m) darker-colored print or solid fabric, we'll call "B"

- Low-loft polyester or poly/cotton blend batting

- Rotary cutter and mat

- Quilting ruler

- Thread to match fabric A

SKILLS

- Strip piecing saves time

- How to add a border to your quilt project

HOW TO SEW CHECKERBOARD PLACEMATS

1 Straighten the cut ends of the fabrics, and trim off the selvages (page 33). Cut five 2½" (6.5 cm) strips from the entire crosswise width of fabric A. Cut five 2½" (6.5 cm) strips from the entire crosswise width of fabric B.

2 Cut seven 2½" (6.5 cm) strips from the entire crosswise width of fabric B, for the border. Cut seven 3" (7.5 cm) strips from the entire crosswise width of fabric B, for the binding.

3 Pin an A strip and a B strip right sides together, aligning the long edges; **insert the pins perpendicular to the long edge** (p. 46). Stitch the strips together, **removing the pins as you come to them** (p. 46). Then stitch another A strip to the other side of the B strip, in the same manner. Continue adding strips, alternating fabrics, until you have three A strips and two B strips. Press the seam allowances **toward the darker fabric** (p. 65) (B).

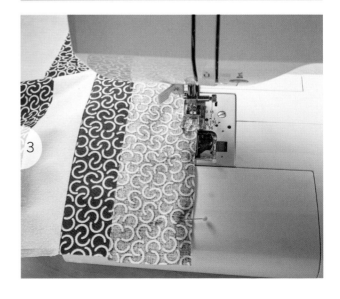

4 Stitch three B strips and two A strips together, as in step 3, with fabrics alternating in the opposite sequence. Press the seam allowances toward the darker fabric (B).

5 Cut the pieced strip sets, perpendicular to the seams, into 2½" (6.5 cm) strips.

✂ **TIP** *If your fabric is 45" (115 cm) wide, you should be able to cut at least seventeen small strips from each set. You will need sixteen of one set and twelve of the other to complete four placemats.*

6 Align the raw edges of two different strips, right sides together, matching the seams. The seam allowances will be pressed in opposite directions. **Insert a pin in the well of the seams** (p. 65), to make sure they line up exactly. Stitch the strips together, removing the pins as you come to them and keeping the seam allowances turned in opposite directions.

(continued)

7 Add five more strips as in step 6, alternating patterns, for a total of seven strips. Press all the new seam allowances in the same direction.

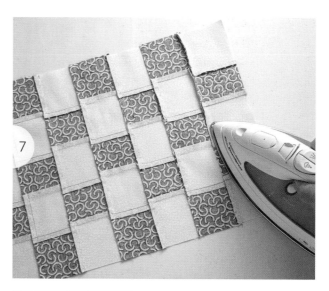

8 **Measure the placemat lengthwise across the middle** (p. 45). Cut two border strips equal to this measurement. Pin one strip to the top of the placemat; pin the other strip to the bottom. Align the ends of the strips to the sides of the placemat. Stretch the strips or the placemat slightly, if necessary, to make them fit. Stitch ¼" (6 mm) seams; press the seam allowances toward the borders.

9 Measure the placemat widthwise across the center, including the new borders. Cut two border strips equal to this measurement. Pin a strip to each side of the placemat, aligning the ends of the strips to the top and bottom edges of the placemat. Stretch the strips or the placemat slightly, if necessary, to make them fit. Stitch ¼" (6 mm) seams; press the seam allowances toward the borders.

10 Repeat steps 6 to 9 for the three other placemats. Cut the backing fabric and batting 4"
(10 cm) longer and wider than the placemat. Layer
and baste the placemats (page 36).

11 Attach a walking foot (page 13). Quilt by
stitching in the ditch (page 43), **following
this sequence**: Begin with a vertical seam near the
center, then a horizontal seam near the center. Then
stitch in the ditch of the seam between the border
and pieced section. Finish by stitching the remaining vertical seams between rows and the remaining
horizontal seams between rows. Bind each placemat,
following the directions on page 44.

tell me more

FOLLOWING THIS SEQUENCE. By quilting
in this sequence, you first anchor the quilt vertically
and horizontally, preventing the layers from shifting.

PIECED SASHING TABLE RUNNER

This table runner, with pieced sashing and quilted motifs, will add a personal decorating touch to your dining room table. The motifs in the center of each square offer an opportunity to practice quilting by hand (page 40). The sashing is made of four hand-dyed fabrics with graduated color values from light to dark. These are often sold in quilt shops, already cut into pieces called "fat quarters." Select a print fabric for the large center squares and the connecting squares of the sashing. Then select four graduating colors that accent the print. The finished size is approximately 52" × 16" (132 × 40.5 cm). All seam allowances for this project are ¼" (6 mm). Select machine-quilting thread in a color to match or blend with the fabrics; select hand-quilting thread (page 24) in a contrasting color.

MATERIALS

- 2 yd. (1.85 m) printed fabric A for large blocks, connecting squares in sashing, backing, and binding

- Four hand-dyed fabrics in fat quarters, or ¼ yd. (0.25 m) each of four full-width fabrics in graduated color values, for the sashing

- Low-loft batting, about 56" × 20" (142 × 51 cm)

- Rotary cutter and mat

- Quilting ruler

- Thread for machine quilting; thread for hand quilting

- Between or sharp hand needle (page 24)

- Heavy paper

SKILLS

- Using fabrics in graduated color values

- Pieced sashing

- Making a quilting template

- Hand-quilting techniques

HOW TO SEW A PIECED
SASHING TABLE RUNNER

1. Straighten the cut edges of your fabrics, and trim off the selvages (page 33). Cut four 8½" (21.6 cm) squares from fabric A; also cut ten 4½" (11.5 cm) squares from fabric A. Cut 2½" (6.5 cm) strips from the entire crosswise width of each of the remaining fabrics; you'll need four strips of each if they are fat quarters or two strips of each if they are 45" (115 cm) wide.

2. Arrange the strips of graduated colors in order from darkest to lightest. Place one strip from the first stack, right sides together, over a strip from the second stack, aligning the long edges. Stitch the strips together. Continue adding strips in graduated sequence from darkest to lightest.

TIP *You can sew these strips together without pinning first if you take your time. Keep the edges aligned and hold both strips with even tension. The strips may not be exactly the same length. Start with the ends evenly aligned and begin stitching from that same end with each additional strip.*

3. Sew the remaining strips into sets like the first one. Press all the seam allowances **toward the darker fabric** (p. 65).

4 Cut the pieced fabric crosswise into 4½" (11.5 cm) strips. You will need a total of 13 pieced sashing strips.

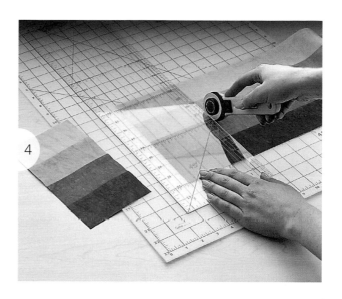

5 Arrange all of the pieces on a flat surface, and step back for a long look. There are many ways you might turn the sashing strips, causing the gradation of color to change direction. You may prefer an arrangement different from the one we have selected.

6 Stitch the long outer rows of sashing strips and **connecting squares** together, keeping the pieces in their arranged order. Press the new seam allowances toward the connecting squares. Return the sashing units to the surface.

tell me more

CONNECTING SQUARES. Often sashing travels uninterrupted from one side of the quilt to the other. However, in this project, the sashing is made up of short pieces alternating with connecting squares. The squares "connect" pieces of the sashing in both directions, while adding an interesting design element.

(continued)

7 Stitch the center row of sashing strips and large squares together, keeping the pieces in their arranged order. Press the new seam allowances toward the squares.

TIP *Pin these pieces together first, one seam at a time, if you prefer. Stitch with the square on top, taking care to keep the seam allowances of the pieced strip turned in the direction they were pressed.*

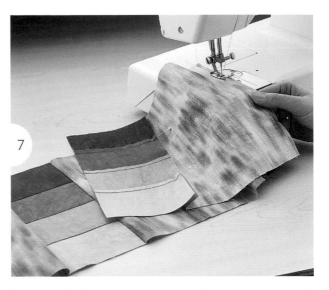

8 Place the bottom sashing row along the lower edge of the center row, with right sides together, matching the seams. The seam allowances will be pressed in opposite directions at the seam intersections. **Insert a pin in the well of the seams** (p. 65), to make sure they line up exactly. Stitch the rows together, **removing the pins as you come to them** (p. 46) and keeping the seam allowances turned in the proper directions.

9 Stitch the remaining sashing row to the other side of the center row, as in step 8. Press these long seam allowances toward the center row.

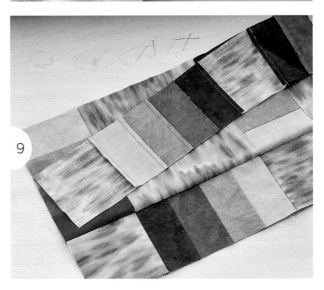

10 Cut a quilting template of the desired shape from heavy paper, approximately 2½" (6.5 cm) tall and wide. Center the template in a connecting square. Trace lightly around the pattern, using a **fabric marker**. Repeat for each of the connecting squares. Trace four intertwined motifs in each large square.

11 Cut the backing and batting 4" (10 cm) longer and wider than the table runner. Layer and baste the table runner (page 36). Quilt by machine, stitching in the ditch (page 43) of the lengthwise sashing seams and all the crosswise seams that run edge to edge. Use a walking foot (page 13).

12 Hand-quilt (page 40) over the marked motifs in each connecting square and in the large squares. Remove your basting stitches. Cut binding strips from fabric A, and bind the table runner (page 44).

tell me more

FABRIC MARKER. Use one of the quilt marking tools shown on page 23 or a water-erasable marker as shown here. Test the marker first on a scrap of fabric to be sure the marks will completely disappear when dabbed with a wet cloth.

FLANNEL CHILD'S QUILT

Create a cozy flannel quilt for your favorite youngster. Begin your fabric selection with a multicolor medium-size print flannel for the sashing and borders. Then, for the strip-pieced sections, select six flannels in colors to coordinate with the print. Pick fabrics of various color values, some in solid colors and others in small prints. You will also need a flannel fabric for the backing. The easy choice would be to repeat one of the strip-piecing fabrics. Ample fabric amounts are given in the materials list because flannel may tend to shrink more than other cotton fabric. All seam allowances are ¼" (6 mm). The finished quilt measures about 55" × 38½" (140 × 98 cm).

MATERIALS

- 1⅝ yd. (1.5 m) fabric, for the sashing and borders

- ⅝ yd. (0.6 m) each of six fabrics that coordinate with the sashing and borders

- 1⅞ yd. (1.75 m) fabric, for the backing (possibly repeat one of the other fabrics)

- Low-loft batting, about 58" × 49" (147 × 125 cm)

- Rotary cutter and mat

- Quilting ruler

- Thread

SKILLS

- Strip-piecing

- Sewing flannel

- Facing instead of binding a quilt

HOW TO SEW A FLANNEL CHILD'S QUILT

1. Straighten the cut ends of the fabric, and trim off the selvages (page 33). Cut two 3" (7.5 cm) strips from the entire crosswise grain of each of the six strip-piecing fabrics. Cut three 3½" × 45½" (9 × 116 cm) sashing strips **from the lengthwise grain** of the sashing/border fabric. Cut four 5½" (14 cm) border strips from the entire lengthwise grain of the sashing/border fabric.

2. Arrange six 3" (7.5 cm) strips in the order you would like to see them in your quilt. Place the first strip over the second strip, right sides together, aligning the long edges. Stitch the strips together. Then stitch the third strip to the other side of the second strip. Continue adding strips in sequence until you have sewn the complete six-strip unit.

3. Sew the remaining strips into an identical six-strip unit. Press all the seam allowances in the same direction. Cut the six-strip units crosswise into 5½" (14 cm) strips. You will need a total of 12 pieced strips. Discard any excess fabric.

4 Stitch three strips together, end to end, in the same sequence, to make one long 18-piece strip. Repeat until you have sewn four identical long strips. Press the new seam allowances in the same direction as the others.

5 Place one sashing strip and one pieced strip right sides together, matching the centers and ends. Pin along the length, easing in any excess fullness. Stitch the seam, removing pins as you come to them and keeping all the seam allowances turned in the same direction.

TIP *It is easiest to sew this seam if the pieced strip is on the bottom, with the seam allowances pressed toward you.*

6 Stitch another pieced strip to the other side of the sashing. Continue until you have stitched all the pieced strips and sashing strips together. Press all the seam allowances toward the sashing strips.

tell me more

FROM THE LENGTHWISE GRAIN. This eliminates the need to piece the sashing and border strips for the lap quilt.

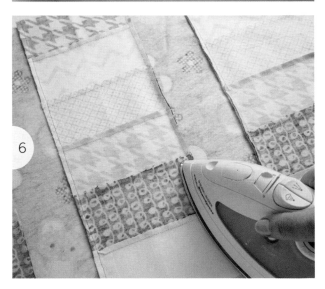

(continued)

7 Measure the quilt top across the middle (p. 45). Cut two of the border strips equal to this measurement. Pin one strip to the top of the quilt; pin the other strip to the bottom. Align the ends of the strips to the outer edges of the quilt top. Stretch the strips or the quilt slightly, if necessary, to make them fit. Stitch ¼" (6 mm) seams; press the seam allowances toward the borders.

8 Measure the quilt top down the middle. Cut the remaining border strips equal to this measurement. Pin a strip to each side of the quilt, aligning the ends of the strips to the edges of the quilt top. Stretch the strips or the quilt slightly, if necessary, to make them fit. Stitch ¼" (6 mm) seams; press the seam allowances toward the borders.

9 Place the quilt top over the backing fabric, and trim the backing fabric to the same size. Layer both pieces, with the backing fabric on top, over the batting. Pin the layers together around the outer edge, using safety pins.

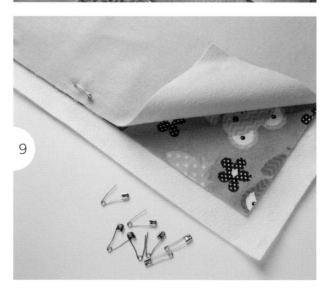

10 With the backing on top, stitch around the quilt ¼" (6 mm) from the edges, leaving a 10" (25.5 cm) opening for turning. Be sure to keep the raw edges of the quilt top and backing even. Trim the batting to ⅛" (3 mm). Trim the corners diagonally, to remove excess bulk. Insert a seam roll or hard cardboard tube into the opening, and place it under the outer seam. Press the seam allowances open.

11 Turn the quilt right side out through the opening. Press lightly around the outer edges. Slipstitch the opening closed, alternating small stitches from one side of the opening to the other.

12 Smooth the quilt out on a flat surface. Baste with safety pins, securing all three layers. Attach a walking foot (page 13). Quilt the lap quilt by stitching in the ditch (page 43) of the border seam. Then stitch in the ditch of the seams between the sashing and the pieced strips, beginning with the center rows and working outward. Remove the safety pins, and the quilt is ready for cuddling.

RAIL FENCE WALL HANGING

Rectangles can be found in dozens of block quilt designs. Here they are recombined in the Rail Fence pattern to create a dynamic wall hanging. A light-to-dark progression of four fabrics accentuates the quilt's zigzag pattern. Select four small prints with color values that progress from dark to light. Or select two solids and two prints that give the same effect. A two-color border, using the two darkest fabrics, creates the illusion of a mat and frame. All of the seam allowances for this project are ¼" (6 mm). Sew as accurately as possible to ensure perfectly matched seams. The finished size is about 38½" × 30½" (98 × 77 cm).

MATERIALS

- ⅜ yd. (0.35 m) fabric A (very light)
- ⅜ yd. (0.35 m) fabric B (light)
- ½ yd. (0.5 m) fabric C (medium)
- 1⅝ yd. (1.5 m) fabric D (dark)
- 1¼ yd. (1.15 m) of muslin, for backing and hanging sleeve
- Batting, about 42" × 32" (107 × 81.5 cm)
- Rotary cutter and mat
- Quilting ruler
- Thread
- Sealed wood lath for hanging the quilt

SKILLS

- Strip-piecing
- Sewing a quilt with a double border

HOW TO SEW A RAIL FENCE WALL HANGING

1 Straighten the cut ends of the fabric, and trim off the selvages (page 33). Cut six 1½" (3.8 cm) strips from the entire crosswise width of each of the four fabrics. Arrange the strips in four stacks (A to D) according to their color value, from lightest to darkest.

2 Pin an A strip and a B strip right sides together, aligning the long edges; **insert the pins perpendicular to the long edge** (p. 46). Stitch the strips together, **removing the pins as you come to them** (p. 46). Then stitch a C strip to the other side of the B strip, in the same manner. Add a D strip to the other side of the C strip. You should now have a pieced set, 4½" (11.5 cm) wide.

3 Repeat step 2 until you have six sets of pieced strips. Press all the seam allowances toward the darkest strips. Cut the strips, perpendicular to the seams, into 4½" (11.5 cm) squares. You should be able to cut at least nine squares from each set; you will need a total of 48 squares to make the wall hanging.

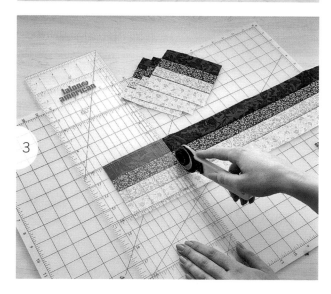

4 Stitch two squares, right sides together, in vertical-horizontal arrangement, with the darkest strips at the right and top. Press the seam allowances toward the vertical dark strip.

5 Stitch two more squares, right sides together, in horizontal-vertical arrangement, with the darkest strips at the top and right. Press the seam allowances toward the vertical light strip.

TIP *Be sure to keep the fabrics in the same sequence from left to right and top to bottom throughout the quilt.*

6 Stitch the two sets, right sides together and seams aligned. **Insert a pin in the wells of the seams** (p. 65), to make sure they line up exactly. Stitch them together, removing the pins as you come to them and keeping the seam allowances turned in the opposite directions. Press the seam allowance toward the lower set.

(continued)

7 Repeat steps 4 to 6 until you have assembled 12 identical blocks. Arrange them in four rows of three blocks, on a flat surface. Stitch each horizontal row of blocks together, matching the seams and keeping the seam allowances turned in the direction they were pressed. Press the seam allowances in the top and third rows toward one side; press the seam allowances in the second and fourth rows in the opposite direction (note arrows). Return them to the flat surface.

8 Place the top two rows right sides together, aligning seams. Stitch, keeping the seam allowances turned in the direction they were pressed. Continue until you have stitched all four rows together.

TIP *Press the quilt top lightly from the right side and then return it to the flat surface. Now, stand back and let your eyes play for a while over the nifty zigzag pattern you have created.*

9 Cut four 1½" (3.8 cm) strips from the entire crosswise width of fabric C, for the inner border. **Measure the quilt top across the middle** (p. 45). Cut two of the border strips equal to this measurement. Pin one strip to the top of the quilt; pin the other strip to the bottom. Align the ends of the strips to the outer edges of the quilt top. Stretch the strips or the quilt slightly, if necessary, to make them fit. Stitch ¼" (6 mm) seams; press the seam allowances toward the borders.

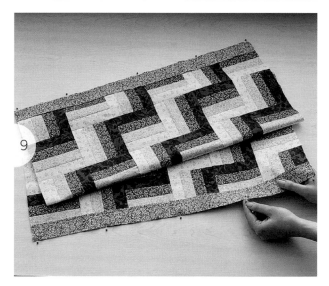

10 Measure the quilt top down the middle. Cut the two side border strips equal to this measurement. Pin a strip to each side of the quilt, aligning the ends of the strips to the edges of the quilt top. Stretch the strips or the quilt slightly, if necessary, to make them fit. Stitch ¼" (6 mm) seams; press the seam allowances toward the borders.

11 Cut four 2½" (6.5 cm) strips from the entire crosswise width of fabric D, for the outer border. Measure for and apply the outer borders in the same manner as the inner borders.

12 Cut the backing fabric and batting 4" (10 cm) longer and wider than the quilt top. Layer and baste the quilt (page 36). Attach a walking foot (page 13). Quilt by stitching in the ditch (page 43), **following this sequence** (p. 73): Begin with a diagonal path near the center, stitching along both sides of the darkest zigzagging strip. Then stitch around both border seams. Finish quilting the remaining zigzagging strips. Bind the quilt (page 44). Add a sleeve for hanging, following steps 20 to 23 on pages 122 and 123.

10

11

12

CHURN DASH WALL HANGING

The simple nine-patch blocks of this Amish-style quilt are made of squares, rectangles, and triangles. The design, symbolic of the mixing movements of an antique butter churn, is created in black fabric and set off by solid, bold, background colors. The triple border frames the design to perfection. Continuous diagonal quilting lines trace the outer corners of all the churn dash blocks and keep the eye moving over the surface of the quilt.

MATERIALS

- ⅝ yd. (0.6 m) black fabric for churn dash design and second border

- ¼ yd. (0.25 m) each of three bold background fabrics

- 1⅓ yd. (1.27 m) for sashing, first and third borders, and binding

- Rotary cutter and mat

- Quilting ruler

- 1⅛ yd. (1.05 m) muslin for backing and hanging sleeve

- Low-loft batting, about 38" (96.5 cm) square

- Thread to match or blend with the fabrics

- Sealed wood lath for hanging the quilt

SKILLS

- Piecing a nine-patch block using a variety of shapes

- Sewing a quilt with multiple borders

- Marking quilting lines on a quilt top

HOW TO SEW A CHURN DASH WALL HANGING

1 Straighten the cut edges of the fabrics and trim off the selvages (page 33). Cut two 2⅞" (7.2 cm) strips on the crosswise grain of the black fabric. From the strips, cut 18 2⅞" (7.2 cm) squares. Cut the squares in half diagonally to make 36 triangles. Also from the black fabric, cut two 2½" (6.5 cm) strips on the crosswise grain. From the strips, cut 36 1½" × 2½" (3.8 × 6.5 cm) rectangles. (You may have to cut a few of the rectangles from strips left over after cutting the squares.)

2 Cut 36 triangles and 36 rectangles from the background fabrics (12 of each color) in the same sizes as the black ones cut in step 1. Cut three 2½" (6.5 cm) squares from each of the background colors for the centers of the blocks.

3 Cut seven 2½" (6.5 cm) strips on the crosswise grain for the sashing and first border. Cut one strip into six 6½" (16.5 cm) pieces for vertical sashing. From the same fabric, cut four 3½" (9 cm) strips on the crosswise grain for the third border and four 3" (7.5 cm) strips for binding. Cut four 1½" (3.8 cm) strips on the crosswise grain of the black fabric for the second border.

4 Place one design and one background triangle, right sides together, aligning all the edges. Stitch ¼" (6 mm) from the long edge, taking care not to stretch the bias edges. Repeat for the remaining 35 pairs, chainstitching one right after the other, without cutting the thread.

5 Place one design and one background rectangle, right sides together, aligning all the edges. Stitch ¼" (6 mm) from one long edge. Repeat for the remaining 35 rectangle pairs, chainstitching one right after the other, without cutting the thread.

6 Clip the triangle and rectangle pairs apart. Press the seam allowances toward the black fabric. Trim off the points that extend beyond the corners of the triangle-pieced squares.

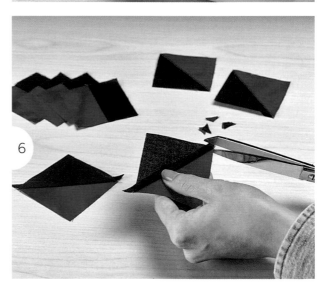

(continued)

7 Arrange the eight pieced squares around the plain center square for each block as shown. Stitch each row of blocks together. Finger-press the seam allowances of the top and bottom rows toward the center. Finger-press the seam allowances of the center row away from the center.

TIP *Clip thread short at the beginning and end of each seam as you go along. This will keep the back of the block looking much neater and prevent long thread tails from getting caught up in the seams.*

8 Place the top row over the middle row, right sides together, aligning the edges and seams. The seam allowances will be pressed in opposite directions. **Insert a pin in the wells of the seams** (p. 65), to make sure they line up exactly. Stitch the rows together, **removing the pins as you come to them** (p. 46) and keeping the seam allowances turned in the opposite directions. Stitch the bottom row to the other side of the middle row in the same manner.

TIP *As you approach seam allowances that have been pressed toward the presser foot, the raw edges may "buckle" under the front of the presser foot. Stop stitching with the needle down in the fabric, and raise the presser foot to allow the seam allowances to return to their pressed position. Use a long pin or the point of your seam ripper to coax them into place and hold them there while you lower the presser foot and continue stitching.*

9 Repeat steps 7 and 8 for the remaining eight blocks. Press the blocks, turning the long seam allowances away from the middle.

7

8

9

10 Arrange the blocks on a surface in three rows of three blocks, following the photo on page 92 or in an order of your own choosing. Place short sashing strips between the blocks in each row. Stitch the first row of sashing strips and blocks together, keeping the pieces in their arranged order. Align the ends of the strips to the upper and lower edges of the blocks, easing the blocks to fit as necessary. It is easiest to stitch with the sashing strip on top, keeping the seam allowances of the block turned in the direction they were pressed.

11 Repeat step 10 for the middle and bottom rows. Check to make sure that the outer points of the black triangles just touch the sashing. If any points are not right, remove the stitches for about 1" (2.5 cm) on each sides of the point, using the point of a seam ripper, and restitch them with the block on top so you can be sure the new stitching line intersects with the point. Press all the seam allowances toward the sashing strips.

12 Return the rows to the work surface. Measure the rows. Cut two sashing strips and two inner border strips to the length of the shortest row. Pin the top border to the top of the top row, easing in fullness evenly. Stitch. Add the sashing to the bottom of the top row. Stitch a border and a sashing strip to the top and bottom of the bottom row.

(continued)

13 Place a straightedge along the first seam between the sashing and block of the top row, extending across the sashing. Make a small mark on the unstitched edge of the sashing next to the straightedge. Repeat at each seam. Pin the middle row to the upper sashing, making sure that the seams align to the marks. Stitch. Join the lower row to the middle row in the same manner.

14 Check the points as in step 11. Correct any that are not perfect. Press the seam allowances toward the sashing and borders. Measure down the center of the quilt and cut the side borders to this length. Pin in place and stitch. Press seam allowances toward the borders.

15 Cut second border strips equal in length to the measurement across the middle of the quilt. Attach the top and bottom borders; press allowances toward the second border. Cut the side borders equal in length to the measurement down the center of the quilt. Attach the side borders; press seam allowances toward the second border.

16 Repeat step 15 for the third border. Spread the quilt out on a flat surface. If you have stitched accurately, the diagonal lines of the churn dash corners will align diagonally across the quilt. You can easily "eyeball" the quilting path in the area of the blocks. Align a straightedge to a one of the diagonal lines and, using a quilt marking pencil, mark the lines extending over the borders. Repeat for the other diagonals in all directions.

17 Layer and baste the quilt as on page 36. Attach a walking foot (page 13). Thread the machine with thread that matches the outer border. Machine-quilt by stitching in the ditch (page 43) of all the border seams. Then stitch along the horizontal sashings. When you quilt the vertical sashings, cross to the opposite side over the horizontal sashings, forming an X at the block corners. Finish by quilting the diagonal lines. Bind the edges, following the directions on page 44. Make a sleeve for hanging the quilt, following steps 20 to 23 on pages 122 and 123.

16

17

FLYING GEESE DOLL BLANKET

Pretty triangles, lined up in rows, echo the V pattern formed by geese as they fly across the sky. Quilted up in dainty pastels, this doll blanket is an exercise in sewing triangles on the bias. The finished size of the blanket is 22" × 16" (56 × 40.5 cm), just right for the popular 18" (46 cm) doll size. Instead of binding, the quilt top is lined to the edge with the backing fabric. Because of its size, this is an easy project to machine-quilt. Even hand-quilting wouldn't take much time. Select a small-scale multicolor floral print fabric for the sashing border, and backing. Then, drawing colors from the print, select three tiny-grained prints in different color values for the "geese" and a white or off-white for the "sky" around them.

MATERIALS

- ¾ yd. (0.7 m) small-scale multicolor print for sashing, borders, and backing
- ¼ yd. (0.25 m) each of three tiny-grained fabrics for geese
- ¼ yd. (0.25 m) white or off-white fabric for sky
- Extra-low-loft batting, about 23 × 17 (58.5 × 43 cm)
- Rotary cutter and mat
- Quilting ruler
- White or off-white thread
- Yarn or pearl cotton in colors to match geese, for tying quilt
- Large-eyed hand-sewing needle for tying quilt

SKILLS

- Chainstitching triangles on the bias
- Pressing bias seams
- Lining to the edge
- Hand-tying a quilt

HOW TO SEW A FLYING GEESE DOLL BLANKET

1 Straighten the cut edges of the fabric and trim off the selvages (page 33). Cut one 5¼" (13.3 cm) strip from the entire crosswise grain of each of the three tiny-grained fabrics. Layer the strips and cut three stacks of 5¼" (13.3 cm) squares. Cut through each stack diagonally in both directions, cutting them into triangles. You will need ten triangles of each fabric. Cut two 2⅞" (7.2 cm) strips from the crosswise grain of the white fabric. Layer the strips and cut sets of fifteen 2⅞" (7.2 cm) squares. Cut each set of squares in half diagonally for a total of 60 triangles.

2 Align the long side of one white triangle to one short side of a colored triangle, right sides together. The points should match at the base of the large triangle. Stitch ¼" (6 mm) from the edge, taking care not to stretch the bias edges. Repeat for the remaining 29 geese, chainstitching one right after the other, without cutting the thread. Place the fabrics in each set in the same direction and stitch the same edges.

3 Clip the units apart. Press the seam allowances toward the small triangles. To avoid stretching the bias edges, move the iron in the direction of the grainline, from the base of the goose toward the point.

4 Stitch a small triangle to the other short side of the large triangle, right sides together, matching the points at the base of the large triangle. Repeat for the remaining 29 geese, chainstitching one after the other. Clip the units apart.

5 Press the seam allowances toward the small triangles, as in step 3. Trim off the points at the tops of the large triangles. Arrange the units on a flat surface in three columns of ten geese as shown.

6 Flip the top unit in the first column over onto the unit below it, right sides together. Turn the set over, so the large triangle of the second unit points to the right and all edges align. Stitch the units together, making sure that the new seam crosses the triangle point **at the exact point where the diagonal seams intersect**.

7 Replace the set on the surface, and continue adding units to the column, following step 6. Repeat for the left column. When you stitch the center column together, you don't have to turn the set over before stitching because the geese are flying in the opposite direction. Place a column facedown on the pressing surface, and slide the iron from one end to the other, pressing all the seam allowances toward the bases of the geese. Repeat for the other columns.

 tell me more

AT THE EXACT POINT WHERE THE DIAGONAL SEAMS INTERSECT. This ensures that the full triangle will be displayed on the right side of the quilt top. If the diagonal seams were sewn accurately at ¼" (6 mm), the intersecting point should be ¼" (6 mm) from the edge. It's OK to cheat a little, if necessary to make the stitches intersect.

(continued)

8 Measure the lengths of the three pieced strips. From the printed fabric, cut three strips on the crosswise grain, 1½" (3.8 cm) wide. From two of the strips, cut pieces for the side borders and sashing equal in length to the shortest pieced strip. Set the other strip aside.

9 Place one sashing strip and one pieced strip right sides together, matching the centers and ends. Pin along the length, **inserting pins perpendicular to the edges** (p. 46) and easing in any excess fullness. Stitch the seam, **removing pins as you come to them** (p. 46) and keeping all the seam allowances turned in the direction they were pressed. Stitch the remaining sashing and side border strips to the pieced strips. Press the seam allowances toward the sashing and borders.

10 **Measure the quilt top across the middle** (p. 45). Cut the top and bottom borders from the remaining 1½" (3.8 cm) strip equal in length to this measurement. Pin the top border strip to the top of the quilt, right sides together, matching the centers and ends. Pin along the length, easing in any excess fullness. Stitch the seam, removing pins as you come to them and keeping all the seam allowances turned in the direction they were pressed. Repeat for the bottom border. Press the seam allowances toward the borders.

11 Place the quilt top over the backing fabric, and trim the backing fabric to the same size. Repeat to cut the batting. Spray the batting with temporary fabric adhesive and apply it to the wrong side of the quilt top. Layer the backing over the quilt top, right sides together. Pin the layers together around the outer edges.

12 With the backing on top, stitch around the quilt ¼" (6 mm) from the edges, leaving a 6" (15 cm) opening for turning. Be sure to keep the raw edges of the quilt top and backing even. Trim the batting to ⅛" (3 mm). Trim the corners diagonally, to remove excess bulk. Turn the quilt right side out through the opening. Press lightly around the outer edges. Slipstitch (page 60, step 12) the opening closed.

13 Smooth the quilt out on a flat surface. Baste with safety pins in the goose columns, securing all three layers. Attach a walking foot (page 13). Machine-quilt by stitching in the ditch (page 43) of the border seam. Or quilt in the ditch by hand (page 40).

(continued)

14 To hand-tie the quilt, thread a large-eyed needle with a double strand of pearl cotton or yarn; don't tie a knot in the end. Take a tiny stitch at the point of the first goose in a column, catching the backing. Pull the strands through, leaving tails about 2" (5 cm) long.

15 Grasp the tails along with the other two strands between the thumb and index finger of your free hand. Wrap the needle end counter-clockwise around the strands and up through the loop that forms.

16 Release the long strands and pull the knot tight to the surface. Trim all tails to the desired length. Tie the quilt at the points of all remaining geese triangles. Remove the safety pins.

MORE FLYING GEESE

Make a matching pillow, using three geese blocks
sewn together in a row; add a narrow border. Use the
border fabric for the backing. Follow steps 12 to 14
on page 67 for making the pillow. Stuff it with leftover
bits of batting.

STAR SASHING LAP QUILT

Sometimes a printed fabric is so lovely, you hate to cut it up. For this lap quilt, sashing strips with connecting stars create splashes of bold color that perfectly complement the whole squares of beautiful floral fabric. Begin fabric selection by choosing an irresistible, multicolor print. Then, from the colors in the print, pick a dark color value fabric for the main sashing and borders. Choose three solid-colors (or small prints that read as solid colors) for the star fabrics that have medium to light values. The final dimensions of this lap quilt are about 35" × 42.5" (89 × 108 cm).

MATERIALS

- ⅝ yd. (0.6 m) multicolor print fabric
- 1 yd. (0.92 m) fabric for sashing strips, borders, and binding
- ¼ yd. (0.25 m) each of three fabrics for stars
- 1 yd. (0.92 m) fabric for backing
- Rotary cutter and mat
- Quilting ruler
- 1 yd. (0.92 m) low-loft batting
- Thread

SKILLS

- Sewing precise triangles
- Matching seams perfectly
- Selecting color-coordinating fabrics for an exciting quilt

HOW TO SEW A STAR SASHING LAP QUILT

1 Straighten the cut edges of your fabrics, and trim off the selvages (page 33). Cut three 6" (15 cm) strips of the multicolor print. From the strips, cut 20 6" (15 cm) squares. Cut five 2¾" (7 cm) strips of the sashing fabric; from the strips, cut 31 6" (15 cm) rectangles.

2 Cut a 2¾" (7 cm) strip from each of the three star fabrics. From each strip, cut four 2¾" (7 cm) squares. Cut two 1⅝" (4 cm) strips from each of the three fabrics. From the strips, cut 32 1⅝" (4 cm) squares of each color.

3 Place a small star square in one corner of a sashing strip, with right sides together and raw edges even. Stitch diagonally as shown.

4 Press the square in half along the stitching line, so the outer edges align to the outer edges of the sashing strip. Trim off the the sashing and under-layer of star fabric at the corner, leaving ¼" (6 mm) seam allowances.

5 Repeat steps 3 and 4 on the other corner of the same end of the sashing strip. Prepare fourteen sashing strips with triangles at one end; five of each of two star colors and four of the remaining color. These will be used as end strips.

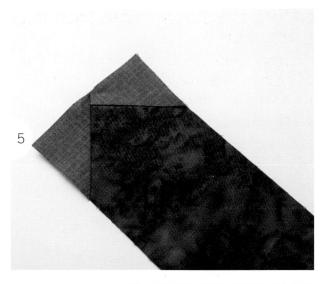

TIP *If you find it difficult to stitch diagonally with accuracy, take the time to draw a light pencil line diagonally on the wrong side of each square. To save time, chainstitch the squares as in step 3 and then do all the pressing and trimming (step 4) at once.*

6 Stitch triangles to all four corners of the remaining seventeen sashing strips, as in steps 3 and 4. Follow the photo in step 13 for color order. These will be used as inner strips.

7 Stitch three end strips between four 6" (15 cm) print squares, using ¼" (6 mm) seam allowances. Make sure all the plain ends align to the tops of the squares. This will be the top row of the quilt. Press the seam allowances toward the print squares. Repeat in the same color order to make a bottom row, with the plain ends of the strips aligned to the bottoms of the squares.

TIP *To avoid confusion and help envision the quilt as it goes together, many quilters mount a large piece of cotton batting on the wall and arrange the pieces on it. (They will stay in place without pins.) The pieces are taken in order as they are stitched and then returned to the batting.*

(continued)

8 Stitch the three inner rows of the quilt together, using the sashing strips that have triangles at both ends, and following the photo in step 13 for color order. Press all the seam allowances toward the squares.

9 Stitch two end sashing strips and two inner strips alternately to the star squares for the first sashing row; follow the photo in step 13 for color order. Stitch with the pieced strips on top so you can make sure the stitches intersect exactly at the points. Press the seam allowances toward the squares. Repeat for the remaining three sashing rows.

10 Arrange all of the pieces on a flat surface. Pin the first row to the first sashing row, right sides together, matching seams. The seam allowances will be pressed in opposite directions at the seam intersections. **Insert a pin in the wells of the seams** (p. 65), to make sure they line up exactly. Stitch the rows together, **removing pins as you come to them** (p. 46) and keeping the seam allowances turned in the proper directions. Stitch with the block rows on top so you can make sure the stitches intersect exactly at the points. Continue adding rows until the entire quilt top is complete. Press all the new seam allowances toward the sashing.

8

9

10

11 Measure the quilt top across the middle (p. 45). Cut two 3½" (9 cm) border strips equal to this measurement. Pin one strip to the top of the quilt; pin the other strip to the bottom. Align the ends of the strips to the outer edges of the quilt top. Stretch the strips or the quilt top slightly, if necessary, to make them fit. Stitch ¼" (6 mm) seams; press the seam allowances toward the borders.

12 Measure the quilt top down the middle. Cut the remaining border strips equal to this measurement. Pin a strip to each side of the quilt, aligning the ends of the strips to the edges of the quilt top. Stretch the strips or the quilt slightly, if necessary, to make them fit. Stitch ¼" (6 mm) seams; press the seam allowances toward the borders.

13 Cut the backing and batting 4" (10 cm) longer and wider than the quilt top. Layer and baste the quilt (page 36). Attach a walking foot (page 13). Quilt by stitching in the ditch (page 43) around each large square, starting with the squares in the center row and working outward to the top and bottom. Bind the quilt, following the directions on page 44.

11

12

13

BOW TIES WALL HANGING

The Bow Tie block has been a favorite of quilters for centuries because of its symmetry and clean geometric lines. The block is made using a simplified method of quick cutting and chainstitching. Begin your fabric selection with a multicolored print for the borders and binding. Drawing colors from this print, select four small coordinating prints or a combination of prints and solids. The wall hanging shown here is made from 16 blocks of each bow tie color. Its finished size is about 37" (94 cm) square.

MATERIALS

- ⅜ yd. (0.35 m) each of four fabrics, A, B, C, and D, for bow ties
- ¾ yd. (0.7 m) background fabric
- ¾ yd. (0.6 m) fabric, for border and binding
- 1¼ yd. (1.15 m) muslin, for backing, plus 6" (15 cm), for hanging sleeve
- Low-loft batting, about 41" (104 cm) square
- Rotary cutter and mat
- Quilting ruler
- Thread that matches one of your fabrics or harmonizes with all of them
- Sealed wooden lath for hanging the quilt

SKILLS

- How to choose several coordinating fabrics
- A new way to piece triangles
- The importance of accuracy in both cutting and piecing
- How to make a sleeve for a hanging quilt

HOW TO SEW A BOW TIES
WALL HANGING

1 Straighten the cut ends of the fabric, and trim off the selvages (page 33). Cut eight 2½" (6.5 cm) strips from the entire crosswise width of the background fabric. From these strips, cut 128 2½" (6.5 cm) squares.

2 Cut two 2½" (6.5 cm) strips from the entire crosswise width of fabric A. From these strips, cut 32 2½" (6.5 cm) squares. Repeat for fabrics B, C, and D, cutting 32 squares of each fabric.

3 Cut two 1½" (3.8 cm) strips from the entire crosswise width of fabric A. From these strips, cut 32 1½" (3.8 cm) squares. Repeat for fabrics B, C, and D, cutting 32 squares of each fabric.

4 Cut eight 3" (7.5 cm) strips from the entire crosswise width of the border/binding fabric: four for the border and four for the binding.

5 Place a 1½" (3.8 cm) square in one corner of a background square, with right sides together and raw edges even. With the stitch length set at 10 to 12 stitches per inch, which equals 2.5 mm, stitch diagonally from corner to corner of the smaller square. Without cutting the thread or removing the first pieced square from the sewing machine bed, repeat this step with a second set of squares. Continue chainstitching in this manner until you have sewn all 128 sets of squares.

6 Lay out the chain of squares on the pressing surface. Press all the small squares in half along the stitched lines, matching the outer edges to the large square.

(continued)

7 Flip the squares over. Trim the large square and one layer of the small square at the stitched corner, leaving ¼" (6 mm) seam allowance. Carefully clip all of the pieced squares apart.

8 With right sides together and raw edges aligned, join a pieced square to a large square of the same bow tie fabric, as shown. Stitch a ¼" (6 mm) seam. Use the chainstitching technique to join all the pieced squares in the same manner.

9 Lay out the chain of joined sets on the pressing surface. Press all the seam allowances toward the whole squares. Carefully clip all the sets apart.

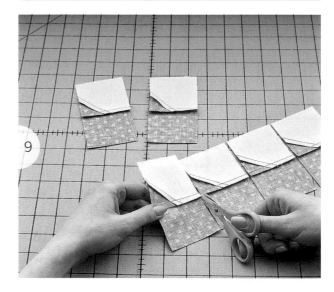

10 Place two similar sets right sides together, aligning the seams at the center. The seam allowances will be pressed in opposite directions. **Insert a pin in the wells of the seams** (p. 65), to make sure they line up exactly. Stitch a ¼" (6 mm) seam, forming a Bow Tie block; remove the pin when you come to it. Use the chainstitching technique to join all the sets into Bow Tie blocks.

TIP *For the first few sets, you may feel more comfortable pinning them together at the center seam. Once you get the rhythm, try stitching them together without the pin. Stitch slowly to ensure that the seams line up perfectly and the seam allowances stay pressed in opposite directions.*

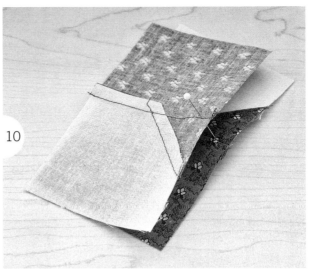

11 Lay out the chain of Bow Tie blocks on the pressing surface. Press all the seam allowances in the same direction. Carefully clip all the blocks apart.

12 Arrange the blocks on a flat surface as shown: eight across and eight down. The seams sewn in step 10 should run vertically, with their seam allowances pressed in alternate directions down each vertical row.

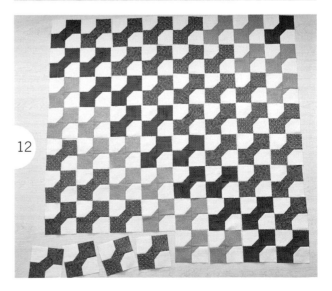

(continued)

13 Join the blocks in one vertical row, stitching ¼" (6 mm) seams, beginning at the top. You should notice that all the aligning seam allowances are pressed in opposite directions (arrows). Press all the new seam allowances in the same direction. Replace the row on the surface.

14 Repeat step 13 for each vertical row, pressing the seam allowances of adjoining rows in opposite directions (arrows).

15 Pin the rows right sides together, aligning raw edges and seams. Again you will notice that all the aligning seam allowances are pressed in opposite directions. Stitch a ¼" (6 mm) seam, removing pins when you come to them.

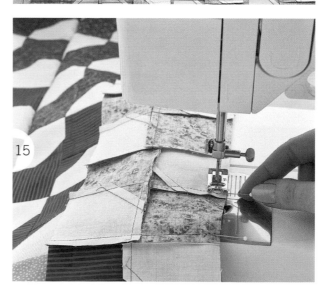

16 Press all the new seam allowances in the same direction (arrows). Lightly press the entire quilt top from the wrong side, then from the right side.

TIP *Now take a little breather. Stand back and admire your work. If you have sewn accurately, all your seams align, forming perfect intersections. That is quite an accomplishment!*

17 **Measure the quilt top across the middle** (p. 45). Cut two of the border strips equal to this measurement. Pin one strip to the top of the quilt; pin the other strip to the bottom. Align the ends of the strips to the outer edges of the quilt top. Stretch the strips or the quilt slightly, if necessary, to make them fit. Stitch ¼" (6 mm) seams; press the seam allowances toward the borders.

18 Measure the quilt top down the middle. Cut the remaining border strips equal to this measurement. Pin a strip to each side of the quilt, aligning the ends of the strips to the edges of the quilt top. Stretch the strips or the quilt slightly, if necessary, to make them fit. Stitch ¼" (6 mm) seams; press the seam allowances toward the borders.

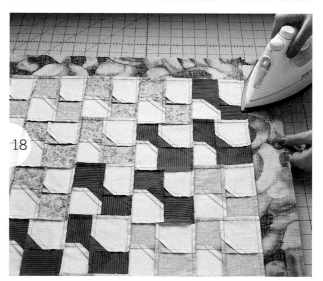

(continued)

19 Cut the backing fabric and batting 4" (10 cm) longer and wider than the quilt top. Layer and baste the quilt (page 36). Attach a walking foot (page 13). Quilt by stitching in the ditch (page 43), **following this sequence** (p. 73): Begin with the center vertical seam; then the center horizontal seam. Then stitch in the ditch of the seam between the border and quilt top. Finish by stitching in the remaining vertical seams between block rows and in the remaining horizontal seams between block rows.

20 Bind the quilt, following the directions on page 44. Cut a piece of washed, unbleached muslin 6" (15 cm) long and the width of the quilt. Fold the short edges under ½" (1.3 cm) twice, and stitch a double-fold hem near the inner folded edge.

21 Fold the strip in half lengthwise, with right sides together and raw edges aligned. Stitch a ½" (1.3 cm) seam and press the seam allowances open. Turn the sleeve right side out; press it flat with the seam centered.

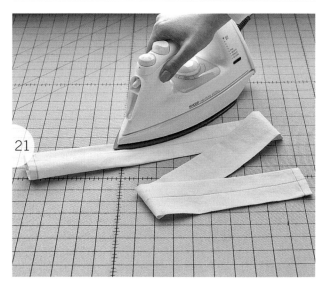

22 Pin the sleeve to the back of the quilt, close to the top edge and 1" (2.5 cm) from the sides. Slipstitch (page 60, step 12) the sleeve to the quilt along the upper and lower edges. Stitch through the backing and into the batting, but don't stitch through to the quilt top.

23 Insert a strip of sealed or painted wooden lath, cut ½" (1.3 cm) shorter than the width of the quilt, through the sleeve. Secure the lath to the wall by sliding the quilt aside and inserting nails or screws ½" (1.3 cm) from the ends of the lath.

22

23

glossary

APPLIQUÉ. This French word refers to a decoration or cutout that is applied to the surface of a larger piece of fabric. Many methods of appliqué are used, including simply machine stitching around the outline of the decoration or hand stitching invisibly.

BIAS refers to the diagonal direction of a piece of fabric. True bias is at a 45 degree angle to both the lengthwise and crosswise grains. Woven fabric has the greatest amount of stretch on the bias.

CHAINSTITCHING. Sewing several individual seams without breaking the stitching threads between the pieces, thus saving time and trips to the ironing board.

COLOR VALUE refers to the relative lightness or darkness of a fabric. In selecting fabrics for a quilt project, it is often necessary to evaluate the color values of various fabrics, both solid colors and prints.

CROSSWISE GRAIN. On woven fabric, the crosswise grain runs perpendicular to the selvages. Fabric has slight "give" in the crosswise grain.

DOUBLE-FOLD HEM. Hems that are made with two folds of equal depths, encasing the cut edge in the crease of the outer fold.

FAT QUARTERS. A half-yard (0.5 m) of fabric, cut down the middle to measure 18" × 22" (46 × 56 cm). This is the equivalent of a quarter-yard (0.25 m) of fabric.

FINGER-PRESS. Rather than use an iron, seam allowances are temporarily pressed to one side with the fingers. This is usually done for bias seams to avoid distortion.

FINISH. To improve the durability of a seam, the raw edge is secured with zigzag stitches that prevent raveling. This is important whenever narrow seam allowances are exposed and must withstand repeated handling or laundering.

GLUE STICK. This temporary fabric adhesive in a plastic tube is a convenient substitute for pinning or basting when you need to hold fabric in place temporarily before stitching. The glue can be applied in small dots. It won't discolor the fabric and can be washed out. It will not harm your machine or gum up your needle as you stitch.

GRAINLINE. Woven fabrics have two grainlines. The lengthwise grainline runs parallel to the selvages. It is the strongest direction of the fabric with the least amount of "give." The crosswise grainline runs perpendicular to the selvages and will "give" slightly when pulled.

LENGTHWISE GRAIN. On woven fabric, the lengthwise grain runs parallel to the selvages. It is the strongest direction of the fabric with the least amount of "give."

LINE TO THE EDGE means that a fabric panel is backed with a lining that is cut to the exact same size. The two pieces are joined together by a seam around the outer edge; the seam allowances are encased between the layers.

LOFT refers to the thickness and springiness of the batting.

MUSLIN. Often used for quilt backings and sleeves on wall hangings or for light background areas in patchwork quilts, this mediumweight, plainweave cotton fabric is relatively inexpensive. Unbleached muslin is off-white with tiny brown flecks; bleached muslin is white.

PIVOT. Perfect corners are stitched by stopping with the needle down in the fabric at the exact corner, before turning the fabric. To be sure the corner stitch locks, turn the handwheel until the needle goes all the way down and just begins to rise.

PRESSING. This step is extremely important to the success of your quilting projects. Select the heat setting appropriate for your fabric and use steam. Lift and lower the iron in an overlapping pattern. Do not slide the iron down the seam, as this can cause the fabric to stretch out of shape, especially on the crosswise grain or bias.

QUILTING HOOP. Similar to an embroidery hoop, this circular or oval, two-piece wooden frame holds the quilt layers taut while you are hand-quilting. An adjustable screw allows you to tighten or loosen the outer hoop to accommodate various thicknesses without crushing the quilt.

QUILTING TEMPLATE. A simple, rigid shape is used as a guide for tracing design lines onto the quilt top for machine or hand quilting. Templates can be cut from firm card stock or translucent vinyl. Ready-made vinyl templates and quilting stencils, also used for marking designs, can be purchased at quilt shops.

SASHING. Strips of fabric, plain or pieced, that are sewn between the square block units of a quilt.

SEAM. Two pieces of fabric are placed right sides together and joined along the edge with stitches. After stitching, the raw edges are hidden on the inside, leaving a clean, smooth line on the outside.

SEAM ALLOWANCE. Excess fabric which lies between the stitching line and the raw edge. Stitching with a narrow ¼" (6 mm) seam allowance is traditional for quilting projects because it minimizes the bulk of fabric behind narrow strips and points.

SELVAGE. Characteristic of woven fabrics, this narrow, tightly woven outer edge should be cut away. Avoid the temptation to use it as one edge of a quilting piece, as it may cause seams to pucker and it may shrink excessively when washed.

STITCHING IN THE DITCH. An easy and often used quilting technique which gives definition to blocks, borders, and sashing. Place the quilt under the presser foot so the needle stitches between two fabrics and into the well of the seam.

STRIP PIECING. Creating pieced designs from long strips of fabric by stitching the strips together and then cutting them crosswise. This method saves time over cutting each piece individually and then sewing them together.

TEMPORARY FABRIC ADHESIVE. Available in a convenient spray can, this product eliminates the need for tedious hand basting. A light layer of this colorless adhesive holds the quilt top, batting, and backing layers together temporarily for machine or hand quilting. The adhesive will not gum up your needle. For some brands the adhesive simply diminishes after a few weeks. For others it can be removed by laundering.

TENSION. When your machine puts the same amount of "pull" on both the top thread and the bobbin thread, your stitches lock exactly halfway between the top and bottom of the fabric layers. Even tension is essential for successful sewing. Some sewing machines require minor tension adjustments when switching from one fabric to another.

ZIGZAG STITCH. In this setting, the needle alternately moves from left to right with each stitch. You can alter the width of the needle swing as well as the length of the stitch. A zigzag stitch that is twice as wide as it is long gives you a balanced stitch, appropriate for finishing the edge of a seam.

index

DON'T MISS THE OTHER BOOKS IN THE SERIES!

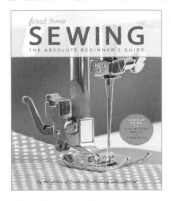

First Time Crochet
Deborah Burger
ISBN: 978-1-58923-825-1

First Time Knitting
Carri Hammett
ISBN: 978-1-58923-805-3

First Time Sewing
Editors of CPi
ISBN: 978-1-58923-804-6

MORE BOOKS ON QUILTING

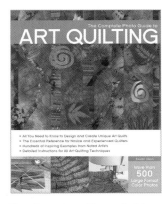

The Quilting Bible, 3rd Edition
Editors of CPi
ISBN: 978-1-58923-512-0

The Quilt Block Book
Nancy Wick
ISBN: 978-1-58923-778-0

The Quilter's Palette
Katy Denny
ISBN: 978-1-58923-799-5

The Complete Photo Guide to Art Quilting
Susan Stein
ISBN: 978-1-58923-689-9

**Creative Publishing
international**

Available online or at your local craft or book store.
www.CreativePub.com